Holy Daring

Holy Daring

THE FEARLESS TRUST
OF ST. THÉRÈSE OF LISIEUX

John Udris

Pauline
BOOKS & MEDIA
Boston

Library of Congress Cataloging-in-Publication Data

Udris, John.
  Holy daring : the fearless trust of St. Therese of Lisieux / John Udris. — 1st U.S. ed.
    p. cm.
  Includes bibliographical references.
  ISBN 0-8198-3389-4 (pbk.)
  1. Thérèse, de Lisieux, Saint, 1873-1897. 2. Christian saints—France—Lisieux—
Biography. I. Title.
  BX4700.T5U37 2007
  282.092—dc22
  [B]

                                    2006033351

Cover design by Rosana Usselmann

Cover photo: © Office Central de Lisieux

Originally published 1997 in England by Gracewing Publishing, 2 Southern Avenue, Leominster, Herefordshire HR6 0QF

Copyright © 1997, 2004, John Udris

First U.S. edition, 2007

Published by Pauline Books & Media, 50 Saint Paul's Avenue, Boston, MA 02130-3491. www.pauline.org

Printed in the U.S.A.

Pauline Books & Media is the publishing house of the Daughters of St. Paul, an international congregation of women religious serving the Church with the communications media.

1 2 3 4 5 6 7 8 9   11 10 09 08 07

Dedicated to Michael and Sean
with deepest gratitude

"*Since, then, we have such a hope,
we act with great boldness.*"

2 CORINTHIANS 3:12

❖

"*I feel within me
a holy daring being born.*"

SAINT THÉRÈSE

Contents

Foreword

ST. THÉRÈSE, that child of light, who in my early years taught me something of her daring trust, never ceases to amaze me with the depth of her insight and wisdom. Her spiritual significance cannot, in my opinion, be overestimated, and most welcome is any book that taps the treasury of her teaching. She can be misunderstood, trivialized. It is evident that the author of this book has listened as a true disciple, really entered into the heart of Thérèse, and here communicates his knowledge of her, writing with conviction. Wisely he concentrates on the mainspring of her life and of her Christian being—trust.

Childlike trust in the God of love revealed in Jesus is the lifeblood of our Christian being, its breath, and not just one virtue among others. Jesus himself never tells us we must love God. Rather, he tells us we must believe and trust God, and surely this is love. To look fearlessly into the Mystery, into Light, inaccessible to human understanding and therefore perceived only as pure darkness and nothing, and to cry: "Abba, dear Father," is the gift of gifts, a sharing in Jesus' own union with his Father. We are children of God, not metaphorically but in utmost reality. It was given to Thérèse to grasp this profound truth, and she labored to bring it to fruition, living out her faith hour by hour. This, alas, is what we fail to do, at least consistently. Udris strikingly illustrates Thérèse's ever-developing insight, her grappling with life's ups and downs. For me personally, her most significant contribution lies in the way she befriended her weakness, her awareness of spiritual inadequacy and failure, and her grasp that all this "poverty," so displeasing and unnerving to us, when really accepted and offered to God, is not a handicap but the springboard into the treasure house of divine Love. The author deals ably with this important aspect of Thérèse's spiritual teaching in chapters 5 and 6. Never did she relax her faith in Abba's loving care for her, no matter how bitter her experience or how unloving, disregarding, and ultimately cruel the divine hands seemed to be.

Thérèse had her own Gethsemane and Calvary. In physical torment, deprived of felt support ("everything has disappeared"), she ultimately tasted defeat: "I can't take any more...I can't take any more...I am reduced." Yet still, with Jesus, she clung to the Abba that was not there and yet was most truly there, affirming with her dying breath: "I am not sorry for delivering myself up to Love."

It seems to me impossible to read this book with care—pondering it page by page, giving full weight to the sensitive selection of the saint's own words—and not share the reaction of her young correspondent, the Abbé Bellière: "You are opening up new horizons for me."

RUTH BURROWS

Acknowledgments

BRINGING THESE PAGES to publication has been made possible only through the generosity of many people. I wish to record my sincere and heartfelt thanks to Sisters Anna and Rachel at Quidenham Carmel, Emma Gilliland, Marie Lamigeon, Alan Bancroft, Reverend Timothy Menezes, and Reverend Derek Lance, who read through the material at various stages and offered helpful suggestions, also to Paul Murray, O.P. and Robert Christian, O.P. for supervising my studies at the Pontifical University of St. Thomas Aquinas, Rome, and who moderated the thesis on which this book is based.

Furthermore, I gratefully acknowledge the following for their permission to use copyrighted material: the Institute of Carmelite Studies, Washington; Cistercian Studies, Michigan; Paulist Press, New Jersey; Ignatius Press, San Francisco; *L'Osservatore Romano* (English Edition), Vatican City; Geoffrey Chapman, London; Harper Collins, London; Sheed and Ward, London; Christopher O'Mahoney, Limerick and Burns and Oates, Tunbridge Wells.

I am much indebted to Ruth Burrows for her foreword, as well as for helping me begin to see how "trust leaps over every obstacle."

Finally, I want to thank my own parishioners at St. Teresa's, Beaconsfield, for their support, kindness, and patience while this book was in preparation.

JOHN UDRIS

Two Sisters in the Spirit: Thérèse of Lisieux and Elizabeth of the Trinity, by Hans Urs von Balthasar. Copyright © 1992 by Ignatius Press, San Francisco.

The New Man, by Thomas Merton. Copyright © 1961 by the Abbey of Our Lady of Gethsemani, Burns & Oates, London.

Aelred of Rievaulx: Mirror of Charity, translated by Elizabeth Connor. Copyright © 1990 by Cistercian Publications, Inc., Kalamazoo, Michigan.

Aelred of Rievaulx: Spiritual Friendship, translated by Mary Eugenia Laker, S.S.N.D. Copyright © 1974 by Cistercian Publications, Inc., Kalamazoo, Michigan.

Athirst for God: Spiritual Desire in Bernard of Clairvaux's Sermons of the Song of Songs, by Michael Casey. Copyright © 1987 by Michael Casey, O.C.S.O, Cistercian Publications, Kalamazoo, Michigan.

Excerpts from *John Ruusbroec: The Spiritual Espousals and Other Works,* from *The Classics of Western Spirituality,* introduction and translation by James A. Wiseman, O.S.B. Copyright © 1985 by James A. Wiseman O.S.B., Paulist Press, Inc., New York/Mahwah, N.J. Used with permission. www.paulist press.com.

Excerpts from *Catherine of Siena: The Dialogue,* from *The Classics of Western Spirituality,* translation and introduction by Susan Noffke, O.P. Copyright © 1980 by Paulist Press, Inc., New York/Mahwah, N.J. Used with permission. www.paulistpress.com.

Excerpts from *Julian of Norwich, Showings,* from *The Classics of Western Spirituality,* translated from the critical text with an introduction by Edmund Colledge, O.S.A. and James Walsh, S.J. Copyright © 1978 by Paulist Press, Inc., New York/Mahwah, N.J. Used with permission. www.paulistpress.com.

Introduction

In Hope of New Horizons

"YOU ARE opening up new horizons for me." This book is about the woman to whom those words were written—Thérèse of the Child Jesus and of the Holy Face. The young man who wrote them was not referring merely to intellectual horizons, some new ideas or insights that she was giving him. He was pointing out the life-changing and emboldening effect of a personal relationship that was fundamentally altering his appreciation of himself, of others, of the world, and especially of God. Such relationships are a remarkable grace. Announcing new opportunities, they push back the boundaries of what formerly seemed possible. Occasioning conversion, they pave the way toward a more abundant life that beckons with a much broader perspective. The consequences of such relationships can be far-reaching, their implications lifelong. There is something holy about the upheaval which they invite. Their impact is of God.

"Do you realize you are opening up new horizons for me?"[1] Found in a letter addressed to Thérèse from a young missionary, these words testify to the vast and vital difference she was making in his life. She had begun to alter his whole outlook, provoking a

---

1. LC 188, in GC II, 1143.

radical reappraisal and reassessment of the way he viewed things. She challenged long-cherished and commonly-held preconceptions, freeing him from their blindfold and thereby expanding beyond measure the parameters of his experience of the living God. In this relationship, at once thrilling and threatening, he sensed that something of immense significance was at stake. Overwhelmed with joy, he felt that something auspicious was unfolding, something all-important under way. The following chapters focus on the nature of the new horizons Thérèse was opening up for him. They carry the conviction that she can do the same for us.

Maurice Bellière was just completing his studies for the priesthood and faced the imminent prospect of being sent on mission to Africa. He had written to the Carmel at Lisieux requesting that one of the sisters be appointed to partner him in prayer. In selecting Thérèse for this task, the mother prioress had chosen someone who was much the same age as this trainee missionary—they were both in their early twenties. Their joint correspondence, over a period of just a year, bears witness to the remarkable transformation wrought by their relationship. The contrast in their characters is unmistakable. Maurice comes across as a diffident young man, earnest and with high ideals, but assailed by self-doubt and lacking in confidence. Thérèse, refreshingly frank and disarmingly honest, teases him out of his timidity. Her words of encouragement are like a "friendly hand...consoling, strengthening, or uplifting,"[2] as he gratefully acknowledges. Often with a lightness of touch and a playful sense of humor, she is able to pick the lock of his imprisoning self-preoccupation to let in some of the clean, fresh air of the Gospel. Her letters come as a revelation to him. They cause a revolution—dispelling fear, instilling trust, engendering hope. Through his contact with Thérèse a new confidence is conceived

---

2. *LC* 189, in ibid., 1150.

within him, and through her influence we sense a new boldness being brought to birth.

The Scriptures have a particular term for this confidence or boldness—*parrhesia.* It is a word that has received little attention until the *Catechism of the Catholic Church* recently recovered and reclaimed it as an important part of the vocabulary of Christian prayer. We wish to explore the meaning of *parrhesia* through the lens of the life and writing of Saint Thérèse of Lisieux. Boldness is the hallmark of her spirituality, the foremost characteristic of her prayer. It pervades her letters, not only to Bellière, but to many others whose horizons she helped to broaden by sharing with them her striking, straightforward appreciation of the Gospel. Her autobiography breathes this boldness, her poetry exudes it, and it forms the recurring theme of many of her last conversations. The testimony of those who knew her reveals how contagious Thérèse's confidence was, and her own novices observed that this was the area of their lives that flourished under her influence and example. We want to discover the source of her fearless trust. How did it develop, and in which furnace was it forged and purified?

Saint Thérèse of Lisieux presents a beautiful profile of biblical boldness—*parrhesia.* She puts flesh and blood on this unfamiliar concept, giving it life and form for contemporary Christians. It's not simply the contours of her spirituality that illustrate the rich content of this New Testament term: she actually seems to embody, in a singular way, evangelical confidence and to epitomize for generations of disciples the multiform dimensions of *parrhesia.*

Thérèse herself was probably unacquainted with this Greek word—indeed, she laments that she did not have the opportunity to learn the original languages in which the Scriptures were written. But she also tells us how, when other spiritual books succeeded only in giving her a headache, one word from the Scriptures was enough to make her mind and heart take flight—"A single word uncovers for my soul infinite horizons."[3] We too hope that this one word, with its wealth of meaning, may provide us with just such a key, which can open up for us further reaches of our Christian faith, widening our field of vision with regard to the rich inheritance we have received. As we come to discover where the term came from and how the members of the Christian community chose to adopt it as their own, we may find that the frontiers of our understanding of the Gospel are expanded and new horizons uncovered, not only in our life of prayer but in every area of our discipleship.

Later we will see how *parrhesia* is particularly associated with praying the Our Father at Mass. In fact, this is the context in which we meet it most often. Used in the introduction to the Lord's Prayer during the liturgy, *parrhesia* translates as: "Let us pray with *confidence* to the Father in the words our Savior gave us." Referring to the words of this sublime prayer, Thérèse once wrote: "What infinite horizons they open to our eyes...."[4] The magnificent dimensions of this prayer are those of the world in which Jesus wants us to live. They are the parameters of the Kingdom in which we experience ourselves to be the beloved sons and daughters of God. They are the horizons of Jesus. Fundamentally, the perspective granted to one who says the Lord's Prayer is that immeasurable expanse constituting what Saint Paul calls "the breadth and length and height and depth"[5]—in other words, the full scale and scope of the Father's love. The Spirit who enables us to pray the Our Father opens up for us this vast panorama. Thérèse's familiarity with these vistas makes us long for the same vantage point. Again and again we shall see that her standpoint is simply the confident trust of a little child. Such childlike directness in her approach to God marked her prayer and made her dare to call him, "Papa," echoing in her native tongue the bold intimacy of Jesus' own "Abba!

---

3. *LT* 226, in ibid., 1094.

4. *LT* 127, in ibid., 724.

5. Eph 3:18.

Father!" The same holy daring animates our praying of the words our Savior gave us.

However, the significance of *parrhesia* has a direct bearing not only on the quality of our engagement with God but on all our relationships. It will become apparent that *parrhesia* concerns the distinctive character of our communication with those around us, especially our closest friends. Exploring the way Thérèse related to her parents and members of her immediate family, to those in her religious community as well as to her correspondents—not least to Bellière—may prompt us to examine more closely the way we communicate with others and in particular the degree of honesty and depth of trust we dare to risk in our relationships. At the same time it can enable us to become aware of the overlap that exists between the way we relate to God and the way we communicate with each other. There is a congruence here. The barriers we erect and the smokescreens we employ in our dealings with others may disconcertingly betray the otherwise hidden or half-guessed dynamics of our relationship with God.

But our theme is still more wide-ranging in its implications and application. In its most primitive New Testament context, *parrhesia* applies to mission. This boldness is a characteristic of the earliest preaching in the Acts of the Apostles. It proved to be the preeminent virtue of the Christian evangelist. How apt, then, that it should be precisely what the would-be missionary Bellière so sadly lacked and so badly needed. How ironic that he should find it in the heart of an enclosed Carmelite who had herself always wanted to be a missionary. And how fitting that she, just thirty short years after her death, should be declared patron saint of the universal missions! By means of his contact with Thérèse, Bellière sensed that this vital aspect to being an evangelist was beginning to emerge in him. In the face of the intimidating dimensions of his missionary endeavor, she was the catalyst for a confidence of similarly mammoth proportions. Subverting his self-doubt and timidity, she was inspiring a trust that promised to surmount every obstacle. She was breathing a boldness into his prayer and preaching—indeed his whole approach to the Christian life—such as he could hardly have imagined.

These, then, were the new horizons she was opening up for him. They are the very horizons we can expect to expand when we enter into relationship with her. The aim of this little book is to afford such an opportunity—to encounter Thérèse. Its ambition is to broker a meeting with this passionate lover of Jesus in the prospect of finding her fearlessness infectious. Its conviction is that her teaching can tap fresh springs of trust within us. Its hope is that we might feel a new current of confidence flooding our prayer, flowing into our relationships, and promising to irrigate every area of our Christian experience. If we yield to the impact of this young woman, we may yet find ourselves among the many whose lives she has overtaken and overturned—decisively. If we allow Thérèse to tutor us in the Gospel, we may rejoice to find ourselves being taken into her confidence—literally. May she partner us in prayer through these pages.

List of Abbreviations

AS   *Autobiography of a Saint* (trans. Ronald Knox), Harvill, London, 1958.

AV   Authorized Version of the Bible.

CCC   *Catechism of the Catholic Church.*

CJ   Carnet Jaune—Pauline's Yellow Notebook in which she recorded some of Thérèse's last conversations. The numerical reference given refers to the date, the month, and the number of the extract.

CL   *Collected Letters of St. Thérèse of Lisieux.*

Conv   *St. Thérèse of Lisieux: Her Last Conversations.*

CR   Counsels and Reminiscences in *Soeur Thérèse: The Little Flower of Jesus.*

GC I   *Saint Thérèse of Lisieux: General Correspondence, Volume I* (1877–1890).

GC II   *Saint Thérèse of Lisieux: General Correspondence, Volume II* (1890–1897).

HA   *L'Histoire d'une Ame* (an early translation of *The Story of a Soul*) in *Soeur Thérèse of Lisieux: The Little Flower of Jesus.*

LC   *Letter to Thérèse.*

LT   *Letter of Thérèse.*

NJB   *New Jerusalem Bible,* Darton, Longman & Todd, London, 1985.

OC   *Thérèse de l'Enfant-Jésus et de la Sainte-Face,* Oeuvres Complètes, Les éditions du Cerf et Desclée De Brouwer, Paris, 1992.

Poems   *Poems of St. Thérèse of Lisieux.*

SS   *Story of a Soul: the Autobiography of St. Thérèse of Lisieux.*

Test   *St. Thérèse of Lisieux by those who knew her:* Testimonies from the
            Process of Beatification.

TEV   *Today's English Version of the Bible,* United Bible Societies of
            America and Collins, London, 1976.

~ *1* ~

Jesus and Thérèse:
Two Icons of Confidence

𝒜 SIGNIFICANTLY new factor in the presentation of the *Catechism of the Catholic Church* is its use of Christian art to enrich the communication of the mystery of our faith. Between its pages we find color plates of frescoes, sculptures, icons, and, in some editions, other works of art that directly relate to the material under discussion. It is striking to notice, first of all, that central to each picture is the figure of Jesus, emphasizing the Christocentric nature of all catechesis. But it is also important to observe how each illustration corresponds to its immediate context, to some extent focusing, and even synthesizing, the subject matter at hand.[1]

The particular work of art introducing "Christian Prayer," the fourth and final section of the *Catechism*, is an eleventh-century painting that depicts Christ standing confidently before the Father, eyes and hands raised in prayer, while his disciples look on. The picture provides the reader of this section of the *Catechism* with the proper focus for all that is to follow. This icon is an open window inviting us to view our subject. And that subject is prin-

---

1. Unfortunately, in one English edition these color plates are slightly out of phase.

cipally a Person. Any consideration of the "what," and the "how," of genuinely Christian prayer cannot begin without an answer to the preeminent question, "Who?" To draw accurately the unique shape of truly Christian praise, adoration, and intercession, we need to trace the lines of our Lord's own relationship with his Father. The prayerful Jesus is our paradigm; he himself is the "master and model of our prayer."[2] Situated purposefully at the threshold of this section of the *Catechism*, the icon bids us to meditate upon Christ's own prayer, contemplating the distinctive features of his own communication with the Father. We are to gaze in wonder at the unique way in which he engages in intimate conversation, letting ourselves be drawn into the mystery of his communion with the Most High. We take our bearings from this definitive point of reference. There is something here that is nonnegotiable, that we can never escape from: "A disciple is not above the teacher...; it is enough for the disciple to be like the teacher" (Mt 10:24–25). The *Catechism* uses the expression "the great practitioners of prayer"[3] —the icon makes it crystal-clear who is chief among them. Jesus alone is the lodestar of this divine dialogue. He is the measure of the methods we employ when we come to pray, and the guarantee of their authenticity. Indeed, "there is no other way of Christian prayer than Christ,"[4] for he himself is its heartbeat, its pulse, its lifeblood. Like the disciples in the painting, we are to look on in order to learn from him that "filial prayer"[5] to which, by grace, we have all become heirs.

Christ's very stance in the painting—his upright posture and even the simple gestures of his raised eyes and his outstretched and open arms—seems to capture and convey an essential characteristic of this "filial prayer" that is the specific subject of our exploration

---

2. *CCC,* 2775.
3. Ibid., 2793.
4. Ibid., 2664.
5. Ibid., 2599, 2605, 2673.

and that is explicitly named in the *Catechism* as *parrhesia*. In the introductory remarks to the section on the Our Father, this "beautiful, characteristically Christian expression," is translated as:

> straightforward simplicity, filial trust, joyous assurance, humble boldness, the certainty of being loved.[6]

The fivefold exposition has been carefully crafted. It captures the manifold and interlocking layers of meaning with which *parrhesia* is laden. So successfully does this fivefold motif embrace our subject, I have incorporated it into the framework of the following chapters. While providing a useful backdrop, these descriptions will also form the perfect outline for a compelling portrait of Saint Thérèse of Lisieux, to which this look at her life and teaching will, with hope, lend color and texture.

From the beginning, however, we need to recognize these descriptions primarily as characteristics of Jesus. In broad brushstrokes they paint the dynamics of his unique way of relating to the Father as well as to those around him. They pinpoint with striking accuracy the key aspects of Christ's own approach and orientation in prayer. The *Catechism* icon recalls that scene from the Gospel in which the disciples have stumbled upon Jesus praying (cf. Lk 11:1–4). They find themselves privileged to witness, with breathtaking immediacy, the astonishing intimacy of his communion with the Father. They are spellbound. What they observe makes them long to share the same experience. They have wandered in on what makes their Master tick, and they want to be let in on his secret. Eagerly they ask him to teach them to pray. According to the evangelist, it is in reply to this request that Jesus entrusts them with the words of the Our Father. The context here is significant. The Lord's Prayer is pioneered in the wake of this glorious discovery of the Son surrendered in the presence of his Father. The words of the Our Father are a sacrament of his perfect surrender.

---

6. Ibid., 2778.

What we see, graphically expressed in the icon, is what those disciples witnessed: boundless confidence in bodily form. The Jesus depicted in this painting is making eye contact with his heavenly Father. Clearly there is in progress a direct and unhampered communication composed of complete openness and utmost abandonment. He has nothing to hide. His prayer appears impressively free and unrestrained: he is standing rather than kneeling, his head is lifted up rather than bowed down, his eyes are open wide rather than shut tight, and he is stepping forward rather than keeping his distance. His whole body language speaks fluently of a candor and confidence that seem to burst from this portraiture. Nothing is withheld. His trust is transparent. Not only is this trust the impulse behind his words; it is their very breath. In giving his disciples the Our Father, Jesus is not merely handing them a formula of words but his own way of being before God, the hallmark of which is "a humble and trusting heart."[7] The painting effectively conveys this, helping us begin to formulate in our mind's eye an image of *parrhesia*. Not only does the icon give us some important clues as to the yet unfamiliar term; it assists us in appreciating its stance-like nature. Such trust is a quality of presence—a characteristic disposition. It is something that must permeate our prayer. Perhaps that is why the concept itself seems to pervade this part of the *Catechism*.

Pope John Paul II referred to the *Catechism* as a "symphony."[8] Taking up the musical metaphor, it might be argued that *parrhesia* comes through powerfully as a recurring melody, the principal theme of the final movement of this great symphony of faith. In the *Catechism*, there are over thirty explicit references to boldness and trust in various combinations, whether "trust without reservation," "trust and confidence," "bold confidence," or "joyful trust."[9] In

---

7. Ibid., 2785.
8. John Paul II, *Fidei Depositum,* in *CCC,* page 4.

order to simplify the fivefold exposition, we can already identify two particular strands that complement each other to formulate this expression with its unique thrust. Fundamentally, *parrhesia* refers to the kind of trust or confidence that is unimpeded because it is pushed to its furthest limits by boldness or fearlessness. It seems, then, that the constellation of meanings surrounding this rich concept best converge in the descriptions *bold confidence* or *fearless trust*. They are the preferred synonyms we have chosen to translate *parrhesia*. Primarily, fearless trust is an aspect of Jesus' own identity and a principal feature of his prayerful approach to the Father. Bold confidence is the characteristically Christian stance in prayer exemplified by Jesus Christ. The section of the *Catechism* entitled "Christian Prayer" clearly teaches what is evident at the outset from its icon: the Lord Jesus himself is preeminently the one who "teaches us filial boldness."[10]

However, the *Catechism of the Catholic Church* also recognizes the many other witnesses, who

> share in the living tradition of prayer by the example of their lives, the transmission of their writings, and their prayer today.[11]

Thus the saints, too, are guides for our growth in prayerfulness. If we reflect on the *Catechism's* fivefold exposition of *parrhesia,* there can be no doubt that, aside from the Lord Jesus, it seems most clearly to paint a convincing portrait of the little Carmelite from Lisieux. Strong grounds exist for such a claim. Hers is the first voice to speak in the final part of the *Catechism* in response to the question "What is prayer?" This is not to be underestimated. It seems Thérèse holds a privileged position in answering that important

---

9. "Filial trust"—*CCC*, 2734, 2738, 2756, 2778, 2830, 2861. "Trust"—2728, 2733, 2741, 2753, 2797, 2828, 2836, 2837. "Assurance"—2778, 2797. "Filial boldness"—2610, 2621, 2777. "Boldness"—2577, 2778. Other combinations—2571, 2579, 2620, 2633, 2739, 2741, 2777, 2819, 2839.

10. Ibid., 2610.

11. Ibid., 2683.

question for contemporary Christians. Her simple words supply the first authoritative description of prayer that forms the prefix to this whole section:

> For me, prayer is a surge of the heart; it is a simple look turned toward heaven, it is a cry of recognition and of love, embracing both trial and joy.[12]

Here the *Catechism* appears to be acknowledging the lasting value of Thérèse's teaching in this area, perhaps even giving her a certain pride of place among "the great practitioners of prayer." But more particularly, the language of *parrhesia* is so evidently the theological vocabulary of Saint Thérèse. "Simplicity," "trust," "boldness" are all words that figure prominently in her dictionary of discipleship. They express, concisely and comprehensively, her understanding of the Gospel.[13] They are the key components of her Little Way. As we will begin to see, the writings of Saint Thérèse are laden with such language, so much so that it can be perceived as paramount in her own development and pivotal to her spiritual doctrine. Progressively, we shall discover how she illuminates each and all of the different dimensions of Christian confidence. Thérèse teaches us the importance of *straightforward simplicity,* advocating an unambivalent and direct approach in our relationship with God. She demonstrates the *filial trust* that should animate our access to the Father in prayer, and that should mark especially our prayers of petition and intercession. She manifests the *joyous assurance* the Gospel would have us bring to the awareness of our weakness, as well as the *humble boldness* we are urged to exercise when weighed down by our sin. Moreover, through our contact with the heart and

---

12. Ibid., 2558.

13. In the original French of the *Catechism* the key vocabulary here is *"simplicité sans detour, confiance filiale, joyeuse assurance, humble audace, certitude d'être aimé."* *Catéchisme de L'église Catholique,* Service des éditions, Conférence des évêques catholiques du Canada, Ottowa, 1992, 2778. It echoes exactly the French of Saint Thérèse.

mind of Saint Thérèse, we cannot but become increasingly conscious of an abiding *certainty of being loved.* This certainty enabled her to call God "Papa!"—and she invites us to make such evangelical certainty our own.

In the autobiographical material of this trustworthy witness to fearless confidence, there is an image that seems to match, with particular poignancy, the *Catechism's* painting of Christ at prayer. Thérèse describes herself as a little bird gazing up confidently at her divine Sun. She likens herself to a fledgling whose feathers have hardly formed, looking toward the sun that symbolizes God, the goal of her desires. Compared to the great saints, represented by the eagles, she feels utterly insignificant and completely unable to reach the heights they inhabit. Yet, far from being disheartened or discouraged by her impotence, she seizes it as the springboard from which to launch her importunate appeal to the divine eagle—Jesus—to lend her his own wings. With them she is supremely confident that she will succeed in her holy ambition. Though the capacity to fly is beyond this little bird, its aspirations are those of an eagle. Thérèse is not tortured by these desires, because she believes they have been planted in her by the Lord in the first place and "God never gives desires that He cannot realize."[14] For Thérèse, not only is God the author of these aspirations, she is sure that they actually comprise the Lord's own desires in her.

In vivid colors this image conveys a powerful message: frailty and fearlessness are not incompatible. In one who is living by grace they can—indeed must—be two sides of the same coin. Furthermore, for all its innocence, Thérèse's story of the bird is not insipid or sentimental. Its simplicity belies its gravity. Such imagery is born of suffering. As we enter into the mystery of this parable, we will find ourselves being taken to where it was composed, to that terrifying, harrowing place where the sun is eclipsed by clouds and

---

14. *LT* 197, in *GC* II, 1000.

darkness covers the land. We will be led to the dereliction and destitution of the cross, where trust is tried and tested. The story will bring us to the heart of the paschal mystery, for this little bird embodies the fearless trust Christ brought to his crucifixion and that Thérèse took to her own passion.

Focusing and synthesizing the subject we have undertaken to explore, this image provides us not only with a useful point of reference, but also with an actual way of bringing to our own prayer all that we will begin to discover. It is another icon we can profitably take with us from the outset to guide our steps. We will frequently revisit this image as our familiarity with the spirituality of Saint Thérèse gradually unfolds in its full meaning and significance. But, like the best of icons, it awaits our participation. There is room for us in it. We are to identify with its aspirations and recognize our own reflection in its mystery. It invites us to take our place "under the rays of the Sun."[15] It ushers us into a kingdom where the reason and reward of filial trust is love alone. It dares us to live in a world where "all is grace."[16]

Coupled together, the icon of Jesus in the *Catechism* and the image of Thérèse as a little bird are complementary. They comprise a compelling diptych upon which to contemplate Jesus and Thérèse—two remarkable icons of Christian confidence. The haunting image of the bird under the rays of the sun captures all the salient features of this fearless trust of Saint Thérèse of Lisieux. It will help us to see that if Jesus is the paradigm of *parrhesia*, then she is a magnificent parable of it. Furthermore, she can be for us its foremost protagonist in our following of the Lord.

---

15. Thérèse's own expression and her favorite image for living by grace. Cf. *LT* CLXXV in *CL*, 284.

16. Cf. *CJ* 5.6.4. in *OC*, 1009.

❧ 2 ❧

Parrhesia:
A World within a Word

Before concentrating our attention explicitly on the person of Thérèse of Lisieux, we will take a closer look at the figurative lens that will bring her features into focus for us, namely, the word *parrhesia*. What are its origins? How did its meaning develop? Why did the first Christians find it such a fitting concept to capture and convey their experience of Jesus and the remarkable difference he had made their lives? This fascinating journey will take us through the Old and New Testaments and into the experience of the early Church. But it actually begins in Greece—where the word originated without any religious connotations at all—in the political arena and in the philosophy of friendship.

Parrhesia (pronounced pa-ray-ZEE-ah) comes from and combines two Greek words: *pan,* meaning "all," as in expressions like "panorama" or "panacea," and *rhesis,* meaning "speech," the root of our word "rhetoric." From these etymological roots we are alerted to the word's most primitive, literal sense—that of "saying all," that is to say, "speaking freely." The *pan* qualifies the *rhesis* describing speech that is unhindered, open, and unreserved.

This term originated in ancient Athenian democracy, where it referred to the "freedom of speech" enjoyed by full citizens. Only the full citizen had the right to speak openly in the public assembly—the *ekklesia*—and expect a hearing. Aliens and slaves, for example, enjoyed no such privilege. That it was a hallmark and highly valued characteristic of Athenian citizenship is well attested in a passage from Euripedes, in which one of his characters says:

> I want my sons to go back to the city of cities, to Athens, and hold their heads high and speak like free men there.[1]

Here *parrhesia* is translated with the expression "speaking like free men," and the important image accompanying this use of the word—that of holding one's head high without shame or embarrassment—will recur in different ways. It is clear from this passage that "free speech" was seen as a privilege directly impacting the quality of life enjoyed by the citizens of a democracy.

However, ambiguity surrounded this highly prized political right, and it was quickly perceived as a mixed blessing—a liability as well as a gift. It acquired associations of "excess" and "doing as one liked," attaching to itself connotations of reckless and dangerous "audacity" and even "shamelessness." These negative undertones added another dimension to the term, acknowledging the double edge inherent in freedom. First, there is the distinction between "liberty" and "license," between "permission" and "permissiveness." We are reminded of the great theme in Saint Paul's Letter to the Galatians: "You have been called to liberty, but be careful lest this liberty provide an opening for self-indulgence..." (5:13, New Jerusalem Bible [*NJB*]). However, the negative connotations of this word would actually contribute to its final Christian meaning. The "audacity," "shamelessness," and "sheer nerve" that

---

1. Euripedes, *Hippolytus,* 420–23, Penguin Classics translation, Middlesex, 1953, 40. Cf. a note in *The Hippolytus of Euripedes, with Introduction and Notes* by W. Hadley, University Press, Cambridge, 1889, 74. *Parrhesia* = "with unfettered lips."

carried such derogatory implications in the original secular context of *parrhesia* would eventually inform and influence its Christian use in a positive way.

The notion of being able to say anything openly in the political arena had its equivalent in the private sphere. *Parrhesia* came to be seen as something that existed between friends who could speak candidly to each other. The term appears often in Greek literature on friendship. According to Socrates, a friend should be able to show forth three important qualities: "understanding, good will, and the readiness to be perfectly frank [*parrhesia*]."[2] The sense here is that true friends can share a relationship that is unhampered by inhibitions. Indeed, trust and intimacy are only possible in a friendship where openness and outspokenness exist.

The secular meaning of *parrhesia* in both the public and the private spheres seems to be best expressed by the simple term "candor." There is a delightful story in one of Aristotle's works about a ruler called Pisistratus, who imposed a tax of one-tenth on all the produce of any given piece of land. During one of his inspections he came across a man called Hymettus, who was digging a very stony plot of ground. When Pisistratus asked what he got out of this piece of land, Hymettus, unaware of whom he was speaking to, replied, "Aches and pains, and that's what Pisistratus should have a tenth of!" The ruler was so taken with the man's "frank speech [*parrhesia*]" he granted him complete tax exemption![3] This story, which, as we shall see, has its counterparts both in the Gospels and in the life of Saint Thérèse, testifies to a candor that can compel, charm, and almost irresistibly enchant. This is *parrhesia*.

Nearly all the occurrences of *parrhesia* in the Greek translation of the Old Testament are to be found in the Wisdom literature.

2. Plato, *Gorgias,* 487a, Penguin Classics translation, Middlesex, 1960, 83.
3. Cf. Aristotle, *Atheniensium Respublica,* 16.1–7, in ed. W. Ross, *The Works of Aristotle,* Vol. X, Clarendon, Oxford, 1921.

One notable exception is its single appearance in the Pentateuch. In Leviticus 26:13, the term is used to describe the way in which God's people are able to walk now that they have been freed from their slavery. It is an important text:

> I am the LORD your God who brought you out of the land of Egypt, to be their slaves no more; I have broken the bars of your yoke and made you walk erect.

The significance of *parrhesia* in this particular context lies in the way it pertains to the deportment of those who are free. Those who have tasted liberation are no longer bowed by the weight of their oppression. They walk upright—literally "with *parrhesia*." Deliverance lends confidence to their demeanor. It clearly echoes the passage from Euripedes, in which the free men of Athens were able to hold their heads high. Here, though, *parrhesia* represents the characteristic disposition of those set at liberty by the Lord God of Israel.

This stance-like quality of *parrhesia* is underlined by certain texts in the Wisdom literature that describe the deportment of a righteous person—who is able to "stand with great confidence" (Wis 5:1) before those who oppose him or her. One particular translation of this verse seems to reinforce the spiritual posture of those who possess this *parrhesia:*

> Then the just man will take his stand with poised confidence to outface his oppressors.[4]

The Book of Job employs the term in two places, which pertain directly to the way a person relates to God in prayer. In 22:26 it is used in a speech by Eliphaz, one of Job's accusers. Here Eliphaz counters Job's feelings of shame and worthlessness before God by promising that if Job repents, nothing will hinder his prayer from

---

4. D. Winston, *The Wisdom of Solomon: A New Translation with Introduction and Commentary,* Doubleday, New York, 1979, 144.

reaching heaven. He can enter God's presence unashamed, with his head held high. This implies that freedom from sin—found through repentance—brings about a change in one's bearing before God. Previously one was full of shame; now one experiences joyful confidence. Thus Eliphaz counsels Job, "Then you will delight yourself in the Almighty, and lift up your face to God." *Parrhesia* appears here as the expression for "delighting" in God. Note, too, that it accompanies the phrase about the confident raising of one's head, reminding us of the Leviticus text and, indeed, of the *Catechism's* icon of Christ at prayer. The expression "delighting in the Almighty" recurs later in the Book of Job. Again it pertains to prayer, and again the Septuagint uses the word *parrhesia.* On this occasion Job himself employs the expression, asking rhetorically in the depths of his discouragement:

> Will God hear their cry when trouble comes upon them?
> Will they take delight in the Almighty? (27:9–10)

Still another translation brings the sense to sharper focus: "has he any confidence before him?"[5] *Parrhesia,* then, is clearly a characteristic of one's being before God and especially applies to one's attitude adopted toward God in prayer. In both texts from the Book of Job *parrhesia* is bound to the certainty of that prayer being heard.

Compared to its scarcity in the Old Testament, the word *parrhesia* in its different forms appears quite often in the New. It occurs most frequently in the Acts of the Apostles and refers consistently to the preaching and proclamation of the Gospel in the sense of speaking boldly and without fear. Significantly, the term is used at the beginning of Acts, in Peter's first sermon on the day of Pentecost, where he declares, "Fellow Israelites, I may say to you confidently [with *parrhesia*]" (Acts 2:29). It extends to the closing

---

5. S. Marrow, "*Parrhesia* and the New Testament," *The Catholic Biblical Quarterly*, 44, 1982, 437, footnote 31.

phrase, which describes Paul's continuing ministry of "proclaiming the kingdom of God and teaching about the Lord Jesus Christ with all boldness [with *parrhesia*] and without hindrance" (28:31). The fearless confidence of the first evangelists provided the impetus behind the missionary expansion of the early Church.

In the Gospels *parrhesia* refers to the way Jesus preached the Kingdom: how he told the disciples "plainly" of his forthcoming passion, death, and resurrection (cf. Mk 8:32), how he spoke without ambiguity (cf. Jn 10:24), in a straightforward way (cf. Jn 16:25, 29), and also "openly," as opposed to in secret (cf. Jn 7:26). This is the most basic use of *parrhesia* within the pages of the New Testament; its more profound, theological sense can be found within the epistles.

A key Pauline text that gives rich insight into *parrhesia* is the Second Letter of Saint Paul to the Corinthians 3:12. As we have already discovered and will continue to see, the concepts with which this word is coupled are very illuminating—particularly in the following passage. The combination of the term and the image of Moses' veiled face is no coincidence:

> Since, then, we have such a hope, we act with great boldness [*parrhesia*], not like Moses, who put a veil over his face....

Saint Paul is contrasting the Old and the New Covenants. When Moses prayed he put a veil over his face. Since the coming of Christ, we can pray "bare-faced." One translation of this verse uses the expression "with uncovered face" to translate *parrhesia*. Immediacy and intimacy with God are now available, far exceeding what was possible before. Under the new "dispensation" (3:8), the veil has been dispensed with, and with it, the distance that it implied. In Jesus all covering-up is cast aside in favor of face-to-face contact, and confidence takes a quantum leap forward.

The *Catechism* cites several texts from the New Testament with reference to *parrhesia*. Three passages in the first letter of Saint John reveal different, yet complementary, dimensions of this disposition in the life of the Christian disciple. In the First Letter of Saint John 3:21 we see the distinctive stance of the believer "before God." As the following verse makes clear, this fearless confidence is reflected in what might be termed the ingenuousness or childlike candor of Christian prayer. This is seconded by the use of the word again in 5:14, where it is clear that *parrhesia* is the radical and remarkable confidence that we have in Christ and that should shape our prayer:

> And this is the boldness [*parrhesia*] we have in him, that if we ask anything according to his will he hears us.

The term is also used in the letter to describe the way a disciple will be able to welcome Christ's coming when he appears as our judge (2:28). The confidence that we possess as Christians means that we will "not be put to shame before him" when the Lord comes again. This connection between *parrhesia* and the *parousia* is underlined later in that same letter, when Saint John describes it as the fruit of the fulfillment of love: "that we may have boldness on the day of judgment" (4:17). Significantly, it is precisely in this context that we find the words "perfect love casts out fear...whoever fears has not reached perfection in love" (4:18). These are words that, as we shall see, Thérèse was fond of repeating, her spirituality bearing eloquent testimony to their wisdom.

The Letter to the Hebrews manifests a still further dimension of this evangelical confidence: it is a consequence of the saving work of Jesus. His high priestly work has given us freedom of access to God, his blood enabling us to enter the sanctuary confidently (Heb 10:19). This important text clearly shows the origin and the purpose of such a gift. Its source is "the blood of Jesus." Its goal is "to enter the sanctuary." A careful reading of the verse reveals that what is being described applies here and now; it is referring to a reality already present. This dimension of *parrhesia*—as our confident approach toward God enabled by Christ—can like-

wise be seen in the Letter to the Hebrews 4:16. Because of the saving ministry of Jesus our High Priest, we are invited to "approach
the throne of grace with boldness [with *parrhesia*]." In both of these
references the context is one of exhortation, the perception being
that the believer possesses *parrhesia* because of what Jesus has
achieved and, therefore, we can and should "approach" (cf. 10:22
and 4:16) without any hesitation or holding back.

Here we have reached the most profound level of the New
Testament's use of the term. The only Pauline use of *parrhesia* cited
by the *Catechism* synthesizes beautifully all that we have seen so far.
It describes "Christ Jesus our Lord" as the one "in whom we have
access to God in boldness [*parrhesia*] and confidence through faith
in him" (Eph 3:12). This text captures the utter openness—that
unhindered relationship and unhampered communication—that is
now possible between ourselves and God through, with, and in
Jesus. It is a fundamental attitude or disposition of the Christian
disciple, expresses most powerfully in the way someone prays.

Little wonder, then, that *parrhesia* entered so readily into the
vocabulary of Christian prayer and found a permanent place there in
direct relation to the Our Father. We still meet this term each time
we celebrate the Eucharist, where its uniquely Christian meaning is
fully expressed in the preface to the Lord's Prayer: "Let us pray with
confidence to the Father in the words our Savior gave us."

In the early Church, the specific association of *parrhesia* with
saying the Our Father is strikingly evident. Gregory of Nyssa, in his
homilies on the Lord's Prayer, refers to the Christian's unheard-of
privilege in being able to name God "Father." He emphasizes the
astonishing familiarity the prayer invites and the special disposition
required to address God in this manner: "What a spirit a man must
have to say this word! What confidence [*parrhesia*]!"[6]

---

6. Gregory of Nyssa, *The Lord's Prayer*, 2, translated and annotated by H. Graef,
Newman, New York, 1954, 38.

The way the Lord's Prayer was actually prefaced in the early liturgies is illuminating. One introduction to the Our Father includes a prayer for this very *parrhesia:*

> And grant, O Sovereign Lord, in Thy mercy that we with freedom of speech [with *parrhesia*]...may venture to call upon Thee the holy God who art in heaven as our Father.[7]

In nearly all these prefaces we become aware of another word strongly associated with the language of *parrhesia:* "venturing" or "daring" to call upon God as Father. The Latin liturgy came to adopt here the verb *audere*—from which we get the word "audacity"—as a direct translation of the concept of *parrhesia.* Even today in the Roman Rite, the words immediately leading into the Lord's Prayer are "*audemus dicere*"—"we dare to say." Like *parrhesia,* the word "daring" contains a paradoxical element, including both a favorable and an unfavorable sense. It reinforces not only the fearless, daring nature of authentic Christian prayer but also its seeming insolence, impudence, and sheer nerve. As we will see, this language also abounds in Thérèse.

In another of the early liturgies, *parrhesia* is paired with the expression we have already come across concerning the "uncovering" of one's face:

> Make us worthy, O our Lord and God, that we may stand before You without blemish, with a pure heart and "with uncovered face" and with *parrhesia,* which You in Your mercy have given to us.[8]

Finding these expressions next to each other again underscores their correspondence. We think of the open countenance of Christ in the *Catechism* icon. We should notice, however, the way this pref-

---

7. Divine Liturgy of the Holy Apostle and Evangelist Mark, the Disciple of Holy Peter, quoted in *The Ante-Nicene Fathers,* Volume VII, Eerdmans, Michigan, 1979, 558.

8. W.C. van Unnik, "The Semitic Background of *Parrhesia* in the New Testament" in *Sparsa Collecta: the Collected Essays, Part two,* NovTSup 30, 1980, 295.

ace also hints at the standing posture that we continue to adopt liturgically when praying the Our Father.[9] Standing, as Christ does in the painting, is the poise of the unabashed, unintimidated person, and it speaks powerfully of the confidence the Christian can have before the face of God. We are reminded of the citizens of Athens holding their heads high, and of the liberated Israelites walking erect. These texts reveal not only how *parrhesia* is the precondition and prerequisite for being able to make the Lord's Prayer our own; they also reinforce that, just as it gave the citizens of Greek democracy the right to stand up and speak freely in the public *ekklesia,* so *parrhesia* gives Christians the right to stand up and dare to call God "Father," in the Eucharistic *ekklesia.*

The *parrhesia* of the Christian disciple then is preeminently a *fearless trust* that is the foremost characteristic of an incredible intimacy we are invited to share as sons and daughters of God in Jesus Christ. It is the Christ-won gift that makes us full citizens in the household of God, and that emboldens us with the outspokenness, the audacity, and, we might say, the sheer nerve to call God our "Abba," addressing him and being able to approach him with boundless confidence. This important concept provides us with both a lens and a prism. The lens will bring into sharp focus the face of a saint, enabling us to concentrate on the distinctive features of the spirituality of Saint Thérèse of Lisieux. But *parrhesia* also provides a prism through which all the constitutive elements of Christian confidence are refracted into the *Catechism's* fivefold spectrum, the different colors of which we are now ready to see beautifully illustrated by the life and teaching of this remarkable woman of faith.

---

9. Ibid., "And make us worthy, O Lord our God, to stand before Thee continually with open countenance, and with the confidence [*parrhesia*] which is from Thee...."

⸱∴ 3 ∾

The Straightforward Simplicity
of Saint Thérèse

*E*VEN A CURSORY acquaintance with Saint Thérèse will have made us aware of the immense value she placed on simplicity in the life of a Christian disciple. It is an important part of her appeal to this present generation. She felt keenly that we have complicated our lives beyond measure, and knew all too well how this severely hampers our ability to live as Jesus taught. Furthermore, she sensed how we have made complexity an alibi, an excuse for mediocrity, and a tactic for delaying the day of our real encounter and its consequent commitment. In our subtlety and sophistication, we have become well-practiced in stalling for time, in putting God off and in parrying the primacy of his call. Ironically, in a culture skilled in the invention of communication devices such as answering machines, we have made ourselves increasingly versatile at screening God's calls and expert at keeping his invitations at bay. Thérèse cuts through all this clutter. She blows the whistle on our increasingly resourceful forms of evasion and avoidance, which keep us so complacent with regard to any immediacy of contact with God or with those in whose lives we share. She clears a highway through the undergrowth of our endless equivocation: "for simple souls there must be no complicated ways."[1]

The word "simplicity" comes from two Latin roots: *semel,* meaning "once," and *plicare,* meaning "to fold." Literally, to be simple is to be "folded once." It stands in stark contrast to its opposite "duplicity"—from *duo* and *plicare* meaning "twice-folded." The image is telling. Thérèse's message: our Christianity has far too many creases. Too many contenders vie for our hearts. So we compromise and compartmentalize, parceling out our loyalty. Ambiguity creeps in, buffering and hiding us. We concede to these competing voices until we have almost succeeded in stifling the Kingdom's clarion call, blunting its impact by our prevarication, cushioning ourselves against its sovereign claim, and making our divided loyalties our best defense. The Scriptures have a special name for this debilitating condition: "double-mindedness," "double-heartedness" (cf. Jas 1:8, 4:8; Ps 12:2).

An episode in the life of Elijah the prophet, to whom Carmelites look for their specific charism, graphically illustrates this concept (1 Kings 18:20–40). The people of Israel had been flirting with the idolatrous worship of Baal. In the limping dance that appears to have been characteristic of that worship, Elijah saw an image of the people's uncertainty of allegiance, indeed of their two-timing the living and true God:

> "How long will you go limping with two different opinions? If the LORD is God, follow him; but if Baal, then follow him" (1 Kings 18:21).

Like her Old Testament father, Thérèse reminds us that ours is a jealous God and that he brooks no rivals. She is a similar prophetic figure calling people from their duplicity to simplicity, to a singleness of heart in their allegiance to the Lord. Like Elijah, who was

---

1. *SS,* 254.

known as the "troubler of Israel," she too stands as a sign of contra-
diction, someone who troubles us, whose chaste heart chastises us,
and whose simplicity can jar like cold air on a raw nerve. Thérèse's
simplicity is her single-mindedness. She does not hedge her bets.
In her we have been given a persuasive example of the biblical beat-
itude of purity of heart, which Kierkegaard conceived of as "will-
ing the one thing." She proves a powerful antidote to the spiritual
dissipation that comes from all our double-dealing, promoting the
real possibility of a "single-minded devotion to Christ" (2 Cor 11:3
NJB). She stands as evidence of the evangelical assertion at the
heart of the Sermon on the Mount: "If therefore thine eye be single
thy whole body shall be full of light" (Mt 6:22, Authorized Version
of the Bible [*AV*]). The word used here literally means "simple"
(the Latin translation has *simplex*). The context clarifies and sharp-
ens the meaning. Jesus is asking where our true treasure is, where
our sights are set, where our overriding allegiance lies. He is warn-
ing against the serving of two masters that clouds our vision. This
"single eye" belongs to one whose gaze is fixed on a focal point,
whose clarity of perception is not impaired by a diffusion of competing interests. Persons commenting on this verse have often seen
it as describing "simplicity of intention," a call to a "one-pointed-
ness" modeled by Jesus' own single-hearted commitment to the
Kingdom, and also a summons to become reflections of the simplicity that is the very nature of God. The French Carmels at the
turn of the last century were perceptibly influenced by the spirit of
the Rhineland mystics, among them John Ruusbroec, who had
written of the almost sacramental power of simplicity of intention
to usher us into the presence of God:

> An intention is pure when it intends only God and all other things
> in relation to God. A pure intention drives out hypocrisy and
> duplicity. It keeps a person in God's presence and free of needless

fear both now and on the Day of Judgment. A pure intention is
that "simple eye" which Christ says will keep a person's entire life
filled with light.[2]

Thérèse's purity of intention is massively apparent in her writings;
she is tenaciously one-pointed. She seeks first the Kingdom of God
(cf. Mt 6:33), which is the center of gravity around which orbits
everything else in her life. Her "simple eye" is exquisitely symbolized by the little bird whose loving gaze is fastened firmly on the
object of its desire.

As we have seen by our acknowledgment of the roots of the
word "duplicity," a close relation of simplicity is truth. It is not
surprising to find in the simplest of people an aversion to deceit and
a passion for truth. Some of Saint Thérèse's last conversations reveal
her as an uncompromising advocate and apostle of all that is true:
"I love only simplicity; I have a horror for 'pretense.'"[3] When challenged about her cheerfulness in the face of suffering, she refutes
the suggestion that her smile might simply be a front. This smile
was not, as is often the case with us, a grin of suppressed panic or
a decoy for one's insecurity. Recalling the incident from the Old
Testament, where Jeroboam's wife goes in disguise to the prophet
Ahijah and is found out, Thérèse retorts, "I never 'pretend,' I'm not
like Jeroboam's wife."[4] Indeed, like the prophet on that occasion,
Thérèse exposes our masquerades with the question, "Why do you
pretend to be somebody you're not?" (cf. 1 Kings 14:6). She sees
herself as one who, like her Lord, is "on the side of truth" (Jn 18:37
NJB)—unlike the cowardly Pilate, who could not bear to hear it or
to face its consequences. Thérèse relentlessly tracks down the truth,
believing that it is always ultimately kind. For her trust and truth

2. John Ruusbroec, *The Spiritual Espousals and Other Works* (trans. James A.
Wiseman, O.S.B.), *Classics of Western Spirituality,* Paulist Press, New Jersey, 1985,
121–2.

3. *CJ* 7.7.4 in *Conv,* 77.

4. *CJ* 11.8.6 in ibid., 146.

are sisters (interestingly, in their origins the two English words have the same root and stem). She trusts ferociously that "the truth will make you free" (Jn 8:32), and that the pain often accompanying it is the blood rushing back into veins that have been starved by the tightness of a tourniquet, or the stinging of eyes too long in darkness adjusting to the light. Witness the ruthless honesty of one of her prayers in which she relinquishes control, trusting in advance whatever she will find on the trail of this truth:

> O my God, I really want to listen to You; I beg You to answer me when I say humbly: What is truth? Make me see things as they really are. Let nothing cause me to be deceived.[5]

Would that we were capable of this kind of fidelity to truth, which carries no insurance in its pocket! Thérèse readily disarms her eyes of their defenses. Open wide, they welcome without fear or guile the approach of the One whose name is Truth. She will not be taken in by appearances or hoodwinked by half-truths; neither do cover-ups survive the searing scrutiny of her gaze. All this she has learned from her Master, whose integrity even his opponents could not argue with: "Teacher, we know that you are sincere, and teach the way of God in accordance with truth, and show deference to no one; for you do not regard people with partiality" (Mt 22:16). Jesus' fury was directed at all that was false. So too with Thérèse. His principal opponents were not sinners but hypocrites—literally, the "actors," those who made of their religion a mask to hide behind. Again and again we find Jesus mercilessly ripping through their role-play. Saint Thérèse is committed to the same cause. On the very day of her death at the age of twenty-four, she was heard to say: "I never sought anything but the truth."[6]

This aspect of *parrhesia*—"truth-speaking"—applied to Thérèse's way of relating not only to God but also to those around

---

5. *CJ* 21.7.4 in ibid., 105.
6. *CJ* 30.9 in ibid., 205.

her. She prompts us to come clean in our relationships across the board: with God, with our neighbor, as well as with ourselves. One of her novices testified to this "need to be absolutely frank."[7] Indeed, it seems that she positively encouraged her novices to be as open as possible with her, even going so far as to reveal to her the grief she sometimes caused them. "With a simplicity which delights me, they tell me all...."[8] On one occasion, after a conversation with another sister, Thérèse looked particularly happy. When asked why, this was her reply:

> She told me the truth about myself...and has made me see how imperfect I am. It was good to hear exactly what she thought of me; it's so rarely you hear the truth about yourself. Usually, it is not a very pleasant experience, of course, but for me it was an absolute delight.[9]

She was well aware of the strategy some people use in personal relationships to try to please everyone. In conscience she could not subscribe to this, sensing that such people-pleasing can too easily compromise the truth in a given situation. Thérèse was quite prepared to be unpopular if truth required it: "If I am disliked it cannot be helped. Let the novices not come to me if they do not want to learn the truth."[10] In one of the epistles of Saint Paul, we see this dimension of *straightforward simplicity* particularly at work. In his Second Letter to the Corinthians, Paul refers to the grief he had caused certain Christians when he refused to overlook a situation that was damaging their community. He chose to speak the unpalatable truth rather than take the line of least resistance and safeguard his popularity. Pulling no punches, his strategy of straight-talking evidently caused no little upset. But Paul defends this outspokenness and "unalloyed" sincerity of approach (1:12

7. *Test,* 274.
8. *SS,* 244.
9. *Test,* 227.
10. *CR* in *HA,* 256.

NJB) as a sign of his love for the Corinthians, inviting them to see that the fact that he can speak to them "with the greatest frankness [*parrhesia*]" (7:4) actually testifies to the quality of their relationship as pastor and people. Here Paul is certainly at his candid best, demonstrating the risks as well as the rewards of such an approach.

Simplicity was the quality Thérèse admired especially in one of her sisters, Céline. In a letter to her, Thérèse had no difficulty in calling this her sister's most endearing disposition: "...It is always simplicity that is presented to me as the distinctive characteristic of your heart...."[11] It delighted her because she knew it delighted the Lord. Thérèse links the two relationships and spells out the significance of this feature found in both: "...how your *docility* and childlike *candor* charm Him! ...They move me most poignantly."[12]

It appears from their joint correspondence that these two sisters enjoyed a very special relationship. One of its marks was that they felt free to say anything to each other. Thérèse writes explicitly of the ease she obviously enjoyed in their relationship, and how she felt she could "say everything" to Celine.[13] We are forcefully reminded here of the literal meaning of the word *parrhesia* and its roots in the philosophy of friendship. In their letters to each other, Céline comes across as a friend as well as a sister. Thérèse will refer to her as "that other *myself*"[14] and "*my soul.*"[15] This echoes the vocabulary of Aelred of Rievaulx, who has left us perhaps the most eloquent account of spiritual friendship in our tradition. He would unashamedly refer to one of his closest and dearest friends as "one-in-heart with me,"[16] naming a true friend "another self."[17] He saw

---

11. *LT* 141 in *GC II*, 784.

12. *LT* CXLVII in *CL*, 238.

13. *LT* 96 in *GC I*, 588.

14. *LT* 90 in ibid., 561.

15. *LT* 83 in ibid., 542.

16. Aelred of Rievaulx, *Mirror of Charity* (trans. Elizabeth Connor), Cistercian Publications, Kalamazoo, Michigan, 1990 (1.34), 106.

17. Aelred of Rievaulx, *Spiritual Friendship* (trans. Mary Eugenia Laker, S.S.N.D.), Cistercian Publications, Kalamazoo, Michigan, 1977 (3.70), 108.

the mark of such a friendship as this openness, this willingness to be utterly frank and "up front" with one another. In one place in his famous treatise on friendship he writes lyrically:

> What joy to have someone to whom you dare to speak on terms of equality as to another self; one to whom you need have no fear to confess your failings; one to whom you can unblushingly make known the progress you have made in the spiritual life; one to whom you can entrust all the secrets of your heart.[18]

Thérèse clearly felt she had someone like this in Céline. Their moving correspondence is certainly a monument to spiritual friendship and to the place of *parrhesia* within such relationships. It is interesting that Aelred likewise acknowledges a coherence and continuity between our friendship with others and our friendship with the Lord. For him, John 15:15 was a significant text in this regard: "I have called you friends, because I have made known to you everything that I have heard from my Father." It was this "saying all" that established Jesus' closest followers as friends. The *parrhesia* that Jesus practiced with the disciples is to be a model for our own friendships.

If Thérèse's relationship with Céline was exceptional, it is apparent from her letters that there were others with whom she felt she could speak candidly as a friend, notably the budding missionary Bellière. Clearly, he seems to have found her directness disarming:

> How kind you are, little Sister, in this simplicity and this openness which charm me while embarrassing me![19]

Can we not hear in these sentiments those also of Jesus, charmed by Thérèse's familiarity with him in prayer? Certainly Bellière found the young Carmelite's direct approach greatly appealing, if at first

---

18. Ibid. (2.11), 72.
19. *LC* 193 in *GC II,* 1172.

a little difficult to handle. His words surely betray at the same time
something similar as regards his own relationship with God and
how Thérèse felt it needed to develop. In his letter to her with
which we began, and in the specific context of the new horizons she
was opening up for him, it was precisely this *straightforward simplicity* to which he was referring:

> In your last letter especially, I find some insights on the mercy of
> Jesus, on the familiarity He encourages, on the simplicity of the
> soul's relations with this great God which had little touched me
> until the present because undoubtedly it had not been presented
> to me with this simplicity and unction your heart pours forth.[20]

It is evident from these lines that the simplicity the two have been
discussing is a distinctive quality of relating to God, which implies
a certain directness and familiarity. What Bellière finds so compelling is Thérèse's straightforward approach to God. She is coach-
ing him in this simplicity, which he finds at once "delightful" and
"astonishing."[21] Furthermore, the way she relates to him makes
that simplicity real. And this is what precipitates the breakthrough. As with the best of teachers, the medium is the message.
It is clear from their correspondence that Thérèse is quite direct
and to the point with Bellière and encourages him to return the
compliment: "I would like you to be *simple* with God, but
also...with me."[22] He tells us explicitly that she was the one who
taught him "to keep nothing hidden."[23] She cajoles him for fearing
he had been indiscreet in asking a rather personal question in one
of his letters. On the contrary, she had felt honored by this indis-
cretion, finding his request quite natural and wanting to answer
him in the most transparent terms with details of her family. It

---

20. Ibid., 1143–4.
21. Ibid., 1144.
22. *LT* 261 in ibid., 1165. Here Thérèse underlines the word "simple."
23. *LC* 191 in ibid., 1158.

seems that her frankness and openness with others was itself a lesson in how we should feel free to be with God. Perhaps our praying can often be far too diffident and discreet. For Thérèse prayer should be, as her Carmelite patron and namesake Teresa of Avila liked to say, "nothing else than an intimate sharing between friends."[24] Thérèse divined, almost instinctively, that prayer was meant to be essentially a "delightful heart to heart,"[25] a privileged time of truth-speaking when God and the soul can come clean with each other.

The refreshing candor that colored both Thérèse's relationship with God and with those around her allowed her often to ride roughshod over the rules for communicating politely, in preference to the direct and winning approach of a child. How revealing is the way she writes at the beginning of the final part of her autobiography, addressing her religious superior—then Mother Marie de Gonzague—in this manner:

> O Mother, pardon my childish simplicity. I feel you will allow me to speak to you without considering what is allowed a young religious to say to her Prioress. Perhaps, at times, I shall not keep within the limits prescribed for subjects, but, dear Mother, I make bold to say it, this is your own fault. I am acting with you as a child because you do not act with me as a Prioress but a Mother.[26]

This is a significant text for many reasons. At the most basic level it shows the kind of relationship Thérèse enjoyed with her superior. Her respect is undoubted, but it does not get in the way of free and frank communication. She will not waste time in wondering "what is allowed." She will not let convention be a barrier to what she wants to say, and she recognizes that this means the likelihood

---

24. Teresa of Ávila, *Life*, 8, 5 in *Complete Works, Volume I* (trans. Kieran Kavanaugh, O.C.D. and Otilio Rodriguez, O.C.D.), Institute of Carmelite Studies, Washington, 1987 (8, 5), 96.

25. *LT* 122 in *GC II*, 709.

26. *SS*, 205–6.

of trespassing boundaries. But she will not let that worry her—she blames the mother prioress for blurring those boundaries herself! Note here the significant use of the verb "to dare," which we will discover again and again in Thérèse's writings. Here the expression—translated as "I make bold to say it"—is literally "I dare to say it," and clearly echoes the words that introduce the Lord's Prayer in the Latin liturgy. If we translate this, then, in terms of her relationship to God, we are at the nub of what is meant by *straightforward simplicity* in prayer. Thérèse does not expend needless energy worrying about the etiquette of what is appropriate to say to God. She comes straight out with it. She feels free to "say all," as in the literal and most primitive sense of the word *parrhesia*. Like a little child she discards decorum and dares to come straight to the point, and, if this appears presumptuous, she places the blame fairly and squarely on God who has first overstepped the boundaries, as it were, and chosen to relate to us in such an intimate way. If she appears to go too far, it is because God in Jesus Christ has gone too far in the first place!

Thérèse makes this approach more explicit elsewhere when speaking specifically about prayer. In the autobiographical passage from which the *Catechism* takes its first authoritative answer to the question "What is Prayer?" Thérèse makes it abundantly clear that

> to be heard it is not necessary to read from a book some beautiful formula composed for the occasion.[27]

What a relief it sometimes is to be released from stale and stilted words. Thérèse openly confesses that the search to find such prayers had often given her a splitting headache! Her attitude is quite refreshingly different. Hers is the straightforward approach of a child whose stammerings are nonetheless guaranteed to gain his or her parents' attention, whose first faltering words mean more than

---

27. Ibid., 242.

the finest composition. Thérèse encourages us to find our own voice
in prayer. There is an immediacy of contact implied here that God
delights in. Simplicity prevents the stagnation of our relations with
the Lord. In one of her prayer-poems she proclaims:

> ...the soul which has simplicity
> Gets—every moment—*You* as Nourishment....[28]

These lines convey a lively sense of the "daily bread" that is to be
our relationship with God and that simplicity fosters. Reminding
us of the manna that fed the Israelites in the desert and had to be
gathered afresh each morning (cf. Ex 16:4–21), Thérèse makes us
conscious of the futility of our efforts to live off either other people's experience of prayer or even yesterday's prayer of our own. Like
one of the birds of the air, she dares us not to gather into barns (cf.
Mt 6:26). She knows that prayer perishes if it is hoarded like that.
Trusting that what is needed will be graciously provided, simplicity works against gathering souvenirs. It promotes sensitivity and
vulnerability, which keep our prayer alive. In the *Story of a Soul,*
Thérèse describes the effect of this *straightforward simplicity:* "Jesus
doesn't want me to lay up *provisions;* He nourishes me at each
moment with a totally new food."[29] At all costs she resists fabrica-
tion, which so easily leads to the fossilization of one's prayer.
Giving readers the benefit of her own personal experience of the
way she approaches prayer, Thérèse writes:

> I say very simply to God what I wish to say, without composing
> beautiful sentences, and He always understands me.[30]

She continues to use the language of simplicity in this context to
refer to prayer not only in terms of speaking, but also of looking. She
describes it so succinctly as "a simple glance directed to heaven."[31]

---

28. *PN* 24, 18 in *Poems.*
29. *SS,* 165.
30. Ibid., 242.

Even when there are no words, this look expresses all—constituting in itself that free and frank communication of love. During the last week of her life, when asked what she was saying to Jesus in her prayer, Thérèse simply replied, "I say nothing to Him, I love Him!"[32] The direct communication of love symbolized by a look is deeper than words. We have already come across this simple gaze in her parable of the little bird, but it is present, in the first place, in the *Catechism's* painting of Christ at prayer. Here we see the simple look of the Lord "directed to heaven." We are reminded of the expression "with uncovered eye" used to translate *parrhesia.* The open eyes of Christ manifest this dimension of Thérèse's teaching on prayer—"saying all," hiding nothing. They are symbols of the utter openness and untrammeled honesty so characteristic of authentically Christian prayer. In that picture, Christ's face is in direct contact with the Father. He stands before him "bare-faced"—we might even say "bold-faced." Jesus' confidence in prayer is somehow convincingly evidenced by this "uncovered face." The Scripture text that employs this expression comes, perhaps significantly, from the letter of Saint Paul that we have already referred to in this chapter. The Apostle has been comparing "the confidence we have through Christ in facing God" (2 Cor 3:4 *NJB*) with how Moses used to approach the presence of God his face covered with a veil. Jesus has taken away the need for this veil. In him such obstructions have become obsolete, a hindrance to be discarded. During another of Thérèse's last conversations, she graphically expressed her desire to stand naked before God:

> If I go among the Seraphim, I *shall not do* as they do! All of them cover themselves with their wings before God; I will be very careful not to cover myself with my wings.[33]

---

31. Ibid.
32. *CJ* 26.9.2 in *Conv,* 228.
33. *CJ* 24.9.7 in ibid., 198.

She wanted nothing to stand in the way of the free flow of communication with God, with whom there is now possible, through Christ, an immediacy and a familiarity never before known. This astonishing intimacy is clearly manifest in Thérèse's own particular devotion to the Holy Face, for which she had such a predilection. Her gaze of faith was riveted on the face of Jesus. His countenance was her "only Homeland."[34] She believed that the more we make ourselves at home with that face, the more we shall resemble it. Thérèse carried close to her heart a pouch with a small piece of parchment inside. On it was a depiction of the Holy Face, together with Thérèse's shortest prayer. Her words were direct, simple, and to the point: "Make me like you, Jesus!" They expressed an overriding desire that her life be a looking glass of God's love, like that of her Lord's. This, too, had previously been the intuition of Saint Paul: we are to reflect the glory of God "with our unveiled faces like mirrors" (2 Cor 3:18 *NJB*). In her *straightforward simplicity,* Thérèse mirrors that glory for us quite magnificently.

---

34. *PN* 20, 3 in *Poems.*

∴ 4 ∵

The Filial Trust of Saint Thérèse

Oh! how I wish I could make you realize what I mean! ...It is trust, and nothing but trust, that must bring us to Love.[1]

*W*RITTEN JUST a year before she died, these words from a letter addressed to her eldest sister and godmother, Marie, leave us in no doubt as to the central place confidence holds in the Little Way of Saint Thérèse of Lisieux. Here we will explore the second, and perhaps most fundamental, description of *parrhesia* in the *Catechism*—*"filial trust."* We will concentrate on some of the events in Thérèse's life that, by her own admission, played an important part in the flourishing of confidence, and we will go on to trace the lines of her trust, specifically in her life of prayer.

The story of her entrance into Carmel is itself revealing, shedding radiant light on our subject. Among all of Saint Thérèse's writings, the first explicit use of the term *"confiance"*—which we usually translate as "confidence" or "trust"—occurs in connection with this particular event. It is well known that she desired permission to enter the Carmel at Lisieux at the age of fifteen. Having

---

1. *LT* CLXXVI in *CL,* 290. I prefer Sheed's translation here. Cf. Patricia O'Connor, *In Search of Thérèse,* Darton, Longman & Todd, London, 1987, 147: "In French *'confiance'* expresses confidence (*confidentia*) or personal trust."

received a firm "no" from the ecclesiastical superior of the Carmel, she had had recourse to the bishop of Bayeux, who would not give a definite answer. Three days after this, Thérèse, together with her father and her sister Céline, left on a pilgrimage to Rome. It is in a letter written from Rome to her aunt that we learn of her daring intention:

> I don't know how I'll go about speaking to the Pope. Really, if God were not to take charge of all, I don't know how I would do it. But I have such great _confidence_ in Him that He will not be able to abandon me; I'm placing all in His hands.[2]

Her account of the papal audience is compelling. In her autobiography, Thérèse recalls first the Mass celebrated with the Pope. Though she is writing some eight years after the event, she can still remember the Gospel of the day. It was from Saint Luke, and included the words, "Do not be afraid, little flock, for it is your Father's good pleasure to give you the kingdom" (12:32). These words struck Thérèse like shafts of bright sunlight. It was as if the Lord had spoken directly to her. She recalls how the surge of trust she experienced on that occasion was accompanied by an ebbing away of her fears:

> I was filled with confidence.... No, I did not fear, I hoped the kingdom of Carmel would soon belong to me.[3]

At the audience itself, despite being expressly forbidden to speak, and breaking all the rules of decorum and etiquette, the fourteen-year-old threw herself at the feet of Pope Leo XIII. She placed her hands on his knees and, eye to eye, "in such a way that my face almost touched his"[4] she made her bold request to enter Carmel.

---

2. _LT_ 32 in _GC I,_ 332. My italics.

3. _SS,_ 133.

4. Ibid., 134. This detail is reinforced in a remark made in the last month of her life, "How many times, too, have I thought that at Rome, my face was reproduced in the eyes of the Holy Father." _CJ_ 19.9 in _Conv,_ 192.

Though his reply was initially disappointing, it is Thérèse's conduct in this incident that is so telling. Relating the episode years later, she admits her audacious behavior. But she adds, "If I had not had this audacity, perhaps I would be still in the world."[5]

The point in recalling her behavior in this letter to another missionary, Adolphe Roulland, was to illustrate for him, from her own life, the truth of the words of Matthew 11:12: "The Kingdom of heaven suffers violence, and only the violent take it away."[6] Thérèse sees herself as one who takes the Kingdom—in this case symbolized by Carmel—by force and by storm. She simply would not take no for an answer. Within a year she had received permission to enter. Such audacious persistence is a hallmark of her whole approach to the spiritual path. We think of the women in the Scriptures whose importunity impressed Jesus so much: the Canaanite woman, who was not going to be cold-shouldered by his initial rebuff (Mt 15:21–28), and the widow whose relentless demands for justice eventually secured the judge's vindication— the alternative being that she would hound him to an early grave! (Lk 18:1–8). Thérèse had clearly inherited some of their effrontery and dogged tenacity, which Jesus found so irresistible. The way she has often been depicted has done her great disservice. This Little Flower is no shrinking violet! She is among "the violent" who claim the Kingdom by storming its gates. She rallies us to the same cause. It is noticeable how often she uses military images in her writings. In one of her poems, explicitly quoting the words of Jesus in Matthew 11:12, Thérèse parades the particular arsenal of weapons with which she rushes to take the Kingdom: poverty, chastity, and obedience. This call-to-arms is the very context in which she describes her "holy daring."[7] When it comes to prayer, Thérèse is no pacifist—she puts up a fight. Like Jacob in the Old

---

5. *LT* 201 in *GC II*, 1017.
6. This is the wording Thérèse uses in her letter.
7. Cf. *PN* 48 "My Arms" in *Poems*.

Testament, she is prepared to wrestle with the Lord and will not let him go until he has blessed her (cf. Gen 32:24–32). In her spirituality, this holy violence is a virtue. It is the violence of love. And she first learned it from the Lord.[8]

Both her personal encounter with the Pope and the wider issue of her entry into Carmel and how she dealt with it tell us much about this forceful, formidable Thérèse. The outspokenness she exhibited in the presence of Leo XIII, almost to the point of sheer impudence, can be seen as a parable of the way she felt drawn to relate to the Lord in prayer. She who had no qualms about grabbing the Pontiff by the knees loved to see her relationship with the Lord in such outrageous and alarming terms as taking-Jesus-by-the-heart. However, even the way she dealt with the obstacles to her entrance into Carmel illuminates another aspect of *parrhesia* that may not be so immediately apparent—that of access. We have already seen how the occurrences of this word, particularly in the Letter to the Hebrews, hinge on the dimension of Christian confidence. In the face of discouragement, Thérèse retains an inner conviction that her entrance into "the kingdom of Carmel" is not barred. This aspect of her character further revealed itself during her trip to Rome; when visiting holy sites such as the Colosseum and the Catacombs, she would often give her guides the slip, finding her way into the most sacred areas that were cordoned off from ordinary pilgrims. Thérèse followed an intuition that told her these areas were not meant to be "out of bounds." She recounts a visit to the Colosseum and her irrepressible desire to touch the soil on which the early Christians had been martyred: "we crossed the barrier where there was an opening.... Papa stared at us, surprised at our boldness."[9] Thus she models for us the Christian confidence

---

8. In one of her letters to Monsignor Hugonin seeking permission to enter the Carmel, referring to Jesus, she had written, "I cannot resist the impulse of His gentle violence." *LT* 38C in *GC I,* 387.

9. *SS,* 130.

that our access to the Kingdom is likewise assured—that the way is wide open for us. Looking back at her life from her deathbed, she teases her sister Pauline for her diffidence, stating impishly, "I haven't any fear of anyone; I have always gone where I pleased. I have always slipped by them."[10] In this way Thérèse manifests the robust assertion of the psalmist, who sings to the Lord:

> With you I can break through any barrier,
> With my God I can scale any wall.[11]

But if this intuition was a part of Thérèse's makeup from her youngest days, when was it first corroborated theologically? In her early years in religious life two retreats seem to have figured greatly in this regard. The first was given in 1890 by a Jesuit, Laurent Blino, who, when told by Thérèse of her desire to be a great saint, seems to have been scandalized by such preposterous presumption. She was undaunted, however, and the following year the retreat was led by a Franciscan, Alexis Prou, of whom during her last months she remarked, "I'm very grateful to Father Alexis; he did me much good."[12] The retreat he gave was something of a watershed with regard to her spiritual development. She says of him in her autobiography:

> He launched me full sail upon the waves of *confidence and love* which so strongly attracted me, but upon which I dared not advance.[13]

The language here clearly conveys the sense of entrusting herself to an impulse she felt profoundly, but which until that point she was still not totally sure was of God. Her elder sister Pauline remembers how, until then, scruples often paralyzed this impetus in Thérèse's spiritual life. But after her retreat she experienced something of a liberation:

---

10. *CJ* 10.7.8 in *Conv*, 85.
11. Psalm 17:30 *The Grail* version, Collins, London, 1963.
12. *CJ* 4.7.4 in *Conv*, 73.
13. *SS*, 174. Thérèse underlined the words "confidence" and "love."

From this retreat onwards her trust in God was complete, and she searched spiritual books for approval of her daring.[14]

/Pauline, who had taken on the role of Thérèse's mother when Madame Martin had died, and who as Mother Agnes of Jesus was Thérèse's religious superior for a time, was an important influence in the life of her youngest sister. Thérèse refers to her as "my visible Jesus,"[15] and credits her with having been the first to sow in her heart "the seed of confidence."[16] As a witness in the process for her sister's beatification, Pauline presents a persuasive picture of Thérèse, particularly with regard to her confidence. She describes it as her special characteristic. The specific word Pauline uses here is enlightening: *élan,* meaning "impulse" or "impetus." It is a word that describes this confidence as a drive, a momentum; as something essentially dynamic. *Filial trust* is the fundamental thrust of Thérèse's whole spirituality.[17] In her testimony, Pauline goes on to record how this confidence was never disappointed and how such unrelenting, unremitting trust consistently colored her sister's prayer, especially her prayer of intercession:

> Her loving confidence in our Lord made her extraordinarily daring in the things she asked him for.[18]

Even before Thérèse's entry into Carmel, we have an insight into how her prayers of petition were stamped with unstinting assur-

---

14. *Test,* 43.

15. *LT* 258 in *GC II,* 1153.

16. *CJ* 29.7.10 in *Conv,* 117.

17. Cf. Conrad de Meester's masterful work *Dynamique de la Confiance: Genèse et structure de la "voie d'enfance spirituelle" de Sainte Thérèse de Lisieux,* Les Éditions du Cerf, Paris, 1969, which has happily been recently reprinted. Here he names this confidence as *"the noyau de la 'petite voie'"* (p. 45). It is clear that he means that it is the hub or central core of her "little way"—the dynamic nucleus of all her doctrine around which everything else turns. A summarized version of de Meester's work appears in English as *With Empty Hands: The Message of Thérèse of Lisieux,* Burns & Oates, Tunbridge Wells, 1987.

18. *Test,* 46.

ance. Her prayer for the conversion of the criminal Pranzini, who had been condemned to death, is well known. Thérèse relates how she was "absolutely confident in the mercy of Jesus"[19] as she begged for a sign of Pranzini's repentance. When she read in the newspaper how, on mounting the scaffold, the condemned man had kissed the crucifix—not just once but three times—she reports how she felt that her prayer had not only been answered but answered "to the letter."[20]

Thérèse records an even more bizarre example of her confidence when it came to intercession, this time after her entrance into the Carmel at Lisieux. She had always desired that her closest sister, Céline, would one day join her there. When she heard that Céline would be attending a family wedding, she became apprehensive. Knowing how good a dancer her sister was, and fearing that this might be the occasion for the advance of a possible suitor, Thérèse confesses shamelessly that she "begged God to *prevent {Céline} from dancing.*"[21] She relates how even this prayer was answered, and in no uncertain terms. The usually competent Céline appears to have been temporarily seized with a serious case of two left feet, leaving her dancing partner covered in confusion. Two years later she entered Carmel! Recalling this episode, Thérèse wrote: "This incident, unique in its kind, made me grow in confidence and love...."[22]

Occurrences such as these served to fuel Thérèse's trust in intercessory prayer. She needed to look no further than her own experience for persuasive evidence of the fact that such trust triggers the miraculous. It led her to an appreciation of the power of petition of the most staggering proportions. She intuited that, through our prayer, we actually share in the work of redemption. We are in part-

19. *SS*, 100.
20. Ibid.
21. Ibid., 176.
22. Ibid.

nership with a God who "wills to do nothing without us."[23] In
some mysterious way he makes the salvation of others depend on
us. Taking Jesus' words, "lift up your eyes and see," from the
Gospel story of the woman of Samaria (cf. Jn 4:7–42; Thérèse's
wording), Thérèse applies them to the apostolate of interceding for
others. We are to lift our eyes and see all the empty places in heaven
that are still waiting to be occupied. Through the power he has
invested in prayer, God seems to be saying to us, "It is up to you to
fill them!" It was for this reason Thérèse came to Carmel: *"to people
Heaven."*[24] She sensed the co-redemptive component inherent in
the Christian vocation. Certain images illustrate her understanding
of the mechanics of intercession. She likens the Christian to a river
pouring itself into the open sea, bringing with it everything it has
encountered in its path. In a similar way, when we in prayer plunge
into the ocean of God's love, all the people who have in any way
become caught up in our lives are simultaneously drawn with us
into those depths.

Perhaps the most renowned image associated with Saint
Thérèse—one that sheds immediate light on her astonishing appreciation of the power of intercession—is that of roses. For Thérèse,
the rose was the flower *par excellence.* In her very first poem, the
Child Jesus is portrayed as a rose, symbolizing the sacrificial love
that would shape his life from the crib to the cross. Primarily, however, the rose represented Thérèse's own love for the Lord and her
surrender to him. During June, traditionally the month of special
devotion to the Sacred Heart of Jesus, she would encourage her
novices to throw rose petals toward the figure of the crucified Jesus
in the courtyard of the Carmel. These petals symbolized the "love
for love" of her motto and the motivating force behind her whole

23. *LT* 135 in *GC II,* 753.
24. *PN* 24, 16 in *Poems.*

spirituality.[25] The unpetalling of a rose and the strewing of its petals were expressive of her giving of self in response to Jesus' own gratuitous self-expenditure. Throwing flowers before the Lord represented for Thérèse all her sacrifices and acts of love, including her intercession for others. This was the indispensable contribution she believed she was making from within the cloister walls to the Church militant and that she was certain was making a vital difference to the world. She had no doubts about the leverage love can exert in prayer. In one poem, she uses this imagery to convey the persuasive, even obligating, power of intercession:

> Throwing of Flowers—it arms me, Jesus! I'm
> Certain that when I fight
> > for saving sinners so,
> I'll win. By these I can
> > disarm You every time—
> > These flowers I throw!!![26]

Roses have continued to symbolize the power of intercession from Thérèse's place in the communion of saints. She herself chose to describe the work that she pledged to pursue after her death in these terms: "It will be like a shower of roses."[27] In taking leave of her beloved Bellière, she wants him to see that her death will not impede her ability to champion his cause. On the contrary, now he will experience the power of her prayer as never before. From her place in glory, she will be nearer to him than ever. Moreover, being nearer to God makes her more advantageous still: "I shall give the good God no rest till He has given me all I want."[28] She who had learned how to corner him by her confidence here on earth would

---

25. On the coat of arms which Thérèse created for herself the motto is "Love is repaid by Love alone"—a quote from Saint John of the Cross (*Spiritual Canticle* 9, 7).

26. PN 34, refrain 2 in *Poems*.

27. *CJ* 9.6.3 in *Conv,* 62.

28. *LT* CCXXIV in *CL,* 351.

continue to "spend [her] heaven"[29] in doing just that on behalf of others. In a letter to Céline years earlier, she had already written her creed, "Let us not grow tired of prayer; confidence works miracles."[30]

We can look even more closely at the prayer of Saint Thérèse and its particular quality of filial trust by focusing on some of the actual prayers in her writings. For clarity we will look at three examples corresponding to the three manuscripts that constitute her autobiography. Manuscript "A" contains her Act of Oblation to Merciful Love. She composed this beautiful prayer on Trinity Sunday 1895 as her ready response to an inspiration received during Mass to offer herself in a definitive way to God's infinite love. In it she begs the Lord: "Be Yourself my *Sanctity!*"[31] In this way she expresses boldly the great ambition of her heart. As if to remind the Lord of his promises and hold him to them, she quotes in this prayer his own words from the Gospel of John, "If you ask anything of the Father in my name, he will give it to you" (16:23). On the strength of such a pledge, she dares to say:

> I am certain, then, that You will grant my desires...and it is with confidence I ask You to come and take possession of my soul.[32]

At this point we do well to acknowledge an important connection between Thérèse's desires and her confidence. Put simply, she sees no discrepancy between our deepest desires and what God desires most deeply to give. God is the origin of those aspirations. In a letter to her sister Marie, in which she names the key as "trust, and nothing but trust," Thérèse goes on to state her conviction that

---

29. This famous expression of Thérèse is to be found in *CJ* 17.7 in *Conv,* 102: "I want to spend my heaven in doing good on earth."

30. *LT* 129 in *GC II,* 729.

31. *SS,* 276. Thérèse underlined the word "Sanctity." She recounts the circumstances that surrounded the composition of this prayer toward the end of *Manuscript "A." SS,* 180–1.

32. Ibid.

"the good God never gives desires that He cannot fulfill."[33] She aspires to be a saint. Because God put that desire there in the first place, he will see to its fulfillment. Indeed, the aspiration itself is a sign that God is disposing us to receive his gifts: "He makes us desire, then grants our desires...."[34] This is the *filial trust* of Saint Thérèse.

Such insight is also at work in the writings of Catherine of Siena, who has been called "the Doctor of Desire." In her writing she conceives of the constraining influence these holy aspirations have on God. Our desires force the divine hand, binding him like a slave's shackles. With regard to our deepest desires, Catherine heard the voice of the Lord attest: "You have bound me with that chain—and I myself gave you that chain."[35] Thérèse, too, sensed God's helplessness in the face of his lovers' longings. Citing the Song of Songs, she describes the Father of Jesus as the One who has freely chosen to be imprisoned by our longings and who allows himself to be held captive by the fluttering of a single hair on our necks (cf. Song 4:9). Commenting on this same verse, John of the Cross, in his *Spiritual Canticle,* had used an image that takes us right back to Thérèse's parable of the little bird: "It is indeed credible that a bird of lowly flight can capture the royal eagle of the heights, if this eagle descends with the desire of being captured."[36] The parable perfectly illustrates this possibility, which turns on the coincidence between our deepest yearning and the longing of the Lord. Its message is that our desires are a place of encounter with the divine. Similarly, Thérèse is convinced of the coherence

---

33. *LT* CLXXVI in *CL,* 290.
34. *LT* CLXXVIII in ibid., 294.
35. Catherine of Siena, *The Dialogue,* 15 (trans. Susan Noffke, O.P.), *Classics of Western Spirituality,* Paulist Press, New Jersey, 1980, 54.
36. John of the Cross, *Spiritual Canticle,* 31, 8 in *Collected Works of Saint John of the Cross* (trans. Kieran Kavanaugh, O.C.D. and Otilio Rodriguez, O.C.D.), Institute of Carmelite Studies, Washington, 1979, 534.

between what we most ache for and what God longs most to lavish upon us. On July 13, 1897, just two and a half months before her death, this overwhelming theological insight is recorded, both in a letter to Bellière and during a conversation with her sister Pauline: "God made me always desire what He wanted to give me."[37]

grace

The whole of Manuscript "B," the second part of Thérèse's autobiography—though ostensibly a letter, again written to her eldest sister—is, in fact, substantially a prayer addressed to Jesus. It gives us privileged insight into the intimacy of her relationship with the Lord. Its style itself reveals the directness of her prayer. Copious exclamation marks seem to express the unreserved communication that she felt she could freely enjoy with him, a conversation untrammeled by the self-conscious strictures of modesty and politeness. A similar abundance of question marks reveals a ruthless honesty few of us dare to risk, lest we receive a reply we cannot bear to hear. She is giving us permission to bring all our unanswered questions to prayer. Even the interruptions in her flow of words marked by a succession of dots—a characteristic of all Thérèse's writing but much more prevalent here—create the sense of a lively, vibrant conversation, breaking off suddenly, changing tack, and then beginning again. These gaps (one of them made of no fewer than eighty-eight points!) give the impression of a communication for which at times words just cannot be found.

The vocabulary here also expresses a great deal. We should neither overlook nor underestimate Thérèse's choice of the familiar *tu* to address Jesus. She dispenses with formalities, striding over convention with a forwardness that is always ready to run the risk of impropriety. She feels free to take such liberties with the Lord, as indeed she did with those to whom she wrote. With both Roulland and Bellière, for example, she presumes early on in their correspon-

---

37. *CJ* 13.7.15 in *Conv,* 94. cf. also *LT* 253 in *GC II,* 1140, "He has always made me desire what He wanted to give me."

dence to call them "brother" rather than "Reverend Father." Why is it that we sense they are honored rather than affronted by this? Likewise Jesus, in the familiarity she assumes with him! Thérèse testifies to the lobbying power of this kind of prayer in which even our sighs are eloquent. "I await only a prayer, a sigh from your heart,"[38] she hears her Lord say, implying that he has invested such heartfelt prayer with a coercion he just cannot resist. Exclamations such as "oh!" and "ah!" punctuate this letter, conveying a further feeling of spontaneity, vitality, and even a sense of those groans too deep for words by which the Spirit intercedes (cf. Rom 8:26):

> Ah! my Jesus, pardon me if I am unreasonable in wishing to express my desires and longings which reach even unto infinity. Pardon me and heal my soul by giving her what she longs for so much![39]

Thérèse readily enunciates her desires, disregarding the fact that she seems to be asking for everything. "I would like" appears no less than sixteen times in the early part of this prayer. Psychology has taught us a great deal in recent years about the importance of knowing and expressing what you want in a good, healthy relationship. Ignatius of Loyola, long before Thérèse, had seen the importance of this in terms of our relationship with God. In his *Spiritual Exercises* a prelude intrinsic to each meditation is to name explicitly "what I want and desire."[40] In the Gospels it is the first question Jesus puts to those who would follow him (cf. Jn 1:38) and the one directed to the blind man of Jericho: "What do you want me to do for you?" (Lk 18:41). Thérèse had no difficulty in telling the Lord exactly what she wanted. Just as she freely admits to a tendency to be demanding in her personal relationships—"I...am too bold in

[margin handwritten note: Po voglio Catherine]

---

38. *LT* 135 in *GC II,* 753.
39. *SS,* 192.
40. Usually referred to by the Latin, *"id quod volo"* (cf. *Spiritual Exercises of St. Ignatius,* 48).

my requests... It is so difficult to keep a happy medium!"[41]—so she
is conscious that her prayer may also seem "unreasonable." But she
shifts the blame for her shamelessly daring prayer fairly and squarely onto the Lord's shoulders.

The language of *parrhesia* is to be found in this prayer. She
speaks explicitly of her "boldness," of her "bold desires" and "bold
surrender." The verb "to dare" appears no less than four times.
Once it is used of the little bird to which she likens herself, and
refers to its daring gaze of faith fixed on the divine sun despite the
darkness. Finally, a fresh awareness of the sheer folly of the Lord's
love leads Thérèse to ask, "How can my confidence, then, have any
limits?"[42] This is the kind of trust without qualifications, with no
"ifs" or "buts" or half-measures—a *filial trust* that she chooses to
describe in the last few lines of her prayer as "total."[43]

In the final pages of Manuscript "C"—written just before
Thérèse was moved to the infirmary and too ill to write any more—
her life story lapses one last time into prayer. Sensing that the time
of her departure from this world is near, she applies directly to herself the prayer of Christ on the eve of his passover. Thérèse chooses
to write out almost in full, as if it were her own, the High Priestly
Prayer—John 17:4–24. She is clearly not simply quoting it, for the
French reads in the feminine. She has adapted it—leaving out what
applies only to Jesus. Thérèse dares to make this prayer her own.
Then, as if astonished by her own temerity, she asks the Lord,
"Perhaps this is boldness?" But she already knows the answer, "No,
for a long time You permitted me to be bold with You."[44]

Again in this prayer she uses the verb "to dare." The first time
it refers to her daring to "borrow" our Lord's own words on the

41. *LT* 180 in *GC II*, 916. She asks her correspondent to pardon this "little
Benjamin's importunities."
42. *SS*, 200.
43. Ibid.
44. Ibid., 255.

night before his passion. Its use with that particular verb is clarified
and strengthened by the choice of the same verb a little later on to
describe how she realizes that in order to love as the Lord loves
(which is what the prayer is all about—cf. Jn 17:23), she must
"borrow" his love. Thérèse's instinct is best summed up in a phrase
that has more poignancy and poetry in the original French: *"c'est
Jésus qui fait tout."*[45] It captures the conviction that all authentic
Christian prayer is his prayer in us. Her borrowing of Christ's
words points to the "borrowing" that must be the whole momentum of our prayer in him. Finally, this is expressed beautifully by
Thérèse's audacious application to herself of the father's statement
to the elder brother in the parable of the prodigal son, "all that is
mine is yours" (Lk 15:31). She emphasizes the word "all" and concludes confidently, "Your words, O Jesus, are mine, then."[46] Such
presumption! Such *parrhesia!* Her bold borrowing of the Lord's own
words, based on the belief that everything that is his is also hers,
comes through in a letter to Bellière, which would have been written at about the same time:

> I can only borrow the words of Jesus at the Last Supper. He can-
> not take offense at this since I am His little spouse and, conse-
> quently, His goods are mine.[47]

Thérèse needed no persuading about what this meant: his degree of
directness in prayer could be hers; the measure of intimacy that
Jesus enjoyed with the Father could be hers; his prayer of tremendous *filial trust*—the touchstone of perfect self-expenditure—could
likewise be hers.

In each of the three prayers we have looked at, love stands out.
Thérèse's Act of Oblation is made as a direct response to the invi-

---

45. *LT* 142, 95 in *OC,* 465. The complete sentence runs, *"c'est Jésus qui fait tout et
moi je ne fais rien."* The translation given in *GC II,* 796, is "it is Jesus who is doing
all in me, and I am doing nothing."
46. *SS,* 256.
47. *LT* 258 in *GC II,* 1152.

tation she experienced to accept God's infinite love. In the prayer that is Manuscript "B," Thérèse discovers that her vocation is to be love in the heart of the Church. The final lines of her own "high priestly prayer" are full of the same love the Lord felt for those he was leaving behind to go to the Father. These prayers demonstrate how inextricably confidence and love are intertwined in Thérèse. One leads inexorably to the other. As she wrote to her sister in the letter with which we began: "It is trust, and nothing but trust, that must bring us to Love." Their symbiosis constitutes the Little Way. They are the two wings of our little bird—Thérèse. How fitting that the very last words of her autobiography—an unfinished sentence written in pencil—should be: "I raise myself to Him by means of trust and love...."[48]

---

48. My translation of *"je m'élève à Lui par la confiance et l'amour...."* Manuscript "C," 37, 1 in *OC,* 285.

⁓ 5 ⁓

The Joyous Assurance of Saint Thérèse

W E HAVE SEEN how Saint Thérèse's giant trust strode over every obstruction in her life of prayer. This should make us eager to discover how evangelical confidence relates to two of the greatest sources of discouragement in Christian discipleship—our weakness and our sin. These are the danger areas that have the greatest power and destructive potential to undermine our confidence as Christians. Thérèse shows us how "*joyous assurance*" when faced with one's weakness and "*humble boldness*" when weighed down by one's sin paradoxically make these very areas the most fertile ground for the growth and flourishing of *parrhesia* in the life of faith. In this she is, again, not only a teacher but an eloquent eyewitness:

> I have always wanted to be a saint. Alas! I have always noticed that when I compared myself to the saints, there is between them and me the same difference that exists between a mountain whose summit is lost in the clouds and the obscure grain of sand trampled underfoot by the passers-by.[1]

In these sentiments Thérèse seems to be one with every woman or man who has ever felt the yawning distance between one's deepest

---

1. *SS*, 207.

aspirations and the disappointing reality of one's weakness and deficiency. She, too, has been taunted and tortured by the breach between what one hopes for and what actually happens to be the case. Faced with this discrepancy, cynicism usually creeps in to defend us, if dismay doesn't get there first. Thérèse chose to face this incongruity with yet more confidence and trust—to outstare it, instead, with her *joyous assurance:*

> Instead of becoming discouraged, I said to myself: God cannot inspire unrealizable desires. I can, then, in spite of my littleness, aspire to holiness.... I must bear with myself such as I am with all my imperfections.[2]

Thérèse was not intimidated by her limitations. She knew the Lord loved her, not despite, but actually in and through them. We shall want to look not only at the way that such *joyous assurance* was unleashed in her own life, but also at how she tried to elicit this same confidence in those entrusted to her care, particularly her correspondents.

Thérèse was a realist. She knew that "no human life is exempt from faults."[3] She was all too well aware of her own. Living in community, at such close quarters with others, cannot but give rise to all kinds of tensions. Thérèse was not immune from any of this. There were those in the Carmel whom she naturally enjoyed, and others whom she freely admits "one would make a long detour in order to avoid."[4] She candidly confesses how there was a certain sister whose words, way of behaving, and character itself Thérèse found *"very disagreeable."*[5] She openly relates how prone she herself was to being touchy, fussy, and stubborn. She knew the impatience one feels when things are not to one's liking, and was as liable to get irritated as any of us. Perhaps the most celebrated example of

2. Ibid.
3. *LT* 226 in *GC II,* 1093.
4. *SS,* 225.
5. Ibid., 222. Thérèse underlined these words.

this concerns the sister whom Thérèse sat nearby in the chapel, the rattling of whose rosary beads grated on her nerves and whose fidgeting tormented her so severely that she often got worked up to fever pitch. She is not reluctant or reticent about revealing such shortcomings to others. On the contrary, in her contact with the members of her community, she is convinced that the admission of her own struggles and defects helps rather than hinders, because others can see that she shares the self-same weaknesses. Then they realize that she understands them *"through experience."*[6] This solidarity is an aspect of her spirituality that speaks powerfully to us who read Thérèse today, lending it credibility. This saint is of the same frail flesh and blood. With her we feel we are struggling in the same arena. Of this aspect of the communion of saints, Thérèse once wrote: "I believe the Blessed have great compassion on our miseries, they remember, being weak and mortal like us, they committed the same faults, sustained the same combats...."[7] Part of Thérèse's appeal, not only as an example but also as an intercessor, is that she has those same credentials.

But the attitude she had toward her own imperfections is what is all-important to grasp. Here it seems Thérèse herself experienced illumination and liberation. Again, the breakthrough appears to have occurred during the retreat led by Alexis Prou. Something he said caused a key to turn in the lock of her understanding, opening a door to a completely different approach to her weaknesses. He simply said that our defects do not disappoint God. This daring idea detonated her imagination:

> Never had I heard that our faults *could not cause God any pain,* and this assurance filled me with joy.[8]

The realization that her weaknesses were neither hurting God nor a hindrance to his love for her wrought a real revolution in Thérèse's

---

6. Ibid., 240. The words "through experience" are underlined.
7. *LT* 263 in *GC II,* 1173.
8. *SS,* 174.

way of thinking, unleashing a new surge of trust and "launching [her] full sail on the waves of *confidence and love.*" A different set of horizons, fundamentally those of the Gospel, profoundly altered her perspective, ushering in a *joyous assurance.* Now she found that she was able to bear with herself, "such as I am."[9] She had discovered for herself the freedom once tasted by Saint Paul—the liberation that comes from being content with, and even actually able to rejoice in, one's infirmities for the full scope they give to God's grace and power in one's life (cf. 2 Cor 12:5):

> I am not disturbed at seeing myself *weakness* itself. On the contrary, it is in my weakness that I glory.[10]

Thérèse had experienced something that seemed to overturn the conventional understanding of the way of perfection, vandalizing and vanquishing forever for her a commonly held conception of the virtuous life. She found utterly bankrupt the approach to the spiritual life as an acquisition of merits. She had given up the struggle to make herself perfect, knowing that this can only ever be God's own gracious work. In fact, the grace that had overtaken her was that described by Paul in his Letter to the Philippians: "I am no longer trying for perfection by my own efforts, the perfection that comes from the Law, but I want only the perfection that comes from faith in Christ" (3:9, *Today's English Version* of the Bible [*TEV*]). With the eyes of the New Testament, Thérèse could see that her weaknesses actually favored her, making certain she could not manufacture her own righteousness. This meant that she was the most apt material for the action of grace. She no longer saw her imperfections as a disadvantage. On the contrary, the "supreme advantage of knowing Christ Jesus" (Phil 3:8 *NJB*) gave her a *joyous assurance,* when faced with her weakness, which countered the prevailing religious climate that seemed to promote such a "huffing

---

9. Ibid., 207.
10. Ibid., 224. Thérèse underlined the first "weakness" in this quotation.

and puffing" approach to spiritual progress. Her lack of achievement didn't disillusion her. She actually enlisted it to intensify her
trust:

> ...after seven years in the religious life, I still am weak and imper-
> fect. I always feel, however, the same bold confidence of becoming
> a great saint because I don't count on my merits since I have *none,*
> but I trust in Him who is Virtue and Holiness.[11]

Among Thérèse's last conversations can be found remarks that
clearly indicate how aware of, and awake to, her weakness she was,
right to the end of her life. These comments also reveal how her
very imperfections caused her not discouragement, but rejoicing.
Her faults were fuel not for self-accusation but surrender. They
were the means by which she redoubled her confidence in the work
of grace. One day, when her sister Pauline was talking about her
own weak points, Thérèse said:

> I have my weaknesses also, but I rejoice in them. I don't always suc-
> ceed either in rising above the nothings of this earth; for example,
> I will be tormented by a foolish thing I said or did. Then I enter
> into myself, and I say: Alas, I'm still at the same place as I was for-
> merly! But I tell myself this with great gentleness and without any
> sadness! It's so good to feel that one is weak and little.[12]

Here she teaches us authoritatively, as the saint who did not
"always succeed," to be gentle with ourselves. She did not let her
defects cause discouragement but learned to love them for the way
they kept her dependent, with the greatest immediacy, moment by
moment, upon God's grace. This is what Thérèse means by being
"little." She would later say explicitly that it is "not to become discouraged over one's faults,"[13] remembering how children often fall
but are too small to hurt themselves very seriously.

---

11. Ibid., 72.
12. *CJ* 5.7.1 in *Conv,* 73–4.
13. *CJ* 6.8.8 in ibid., 139.

She tried to convey to others prone to being saddened and dismayed by their weaknesses the following: love your littleness, "love your powerlessness."[14] In a letter to her eldest sister and godmother, who seems to have been in awe of Thérèse's sanctity and unsure that she could ever love Jesus in the same way, Thérèse replies reassuringly:

> What pleases Him is *that He sees me loving my littleness* and my *poverty, the blind hope that I have in His mercy*.... That is my only treasure, dear Godmother, why would this treasure not be yours?[15]

Here is a holiness accessible to us all. If her simplicity demonstrates her purity of heart, Thérèse's *joyous assurance* is the evidence of her poverty of spirit, which rejoices in the recognition that the more we are lacking, the more we actually qualify for the life of the Gospel. Or, as Thérèse herself puts it, "the weaker one is...the more suited one is."[16] To all who would walk that path, and who want to love Jesus in the same way, she counsels: "Let us love our littleness."[17]

To Marie Guérin, a cousin who was experiencing profound discouragement in her prayer and felt she was at an impasse in her spiritual life, Thérèse tried to give a similar perspective. She wanted to prevent Marie from being intimidated by the situation and instead to embrace it, to profit from it, and even to exploit its hidden grace. She teases her cousin, saying that she sounds like a country girl who, when asked by a king for her hand in marriage, wouldn't dare to accept because she has nothing to offer him in return—not realizing that he knows the extent of her poverty much better than she does herself. How often we delay the day of acceptance, thinking to make ourselves more worthy first. Thérèse tries to show her cousin that such a focus is futile and only bound

---

14. One of Thérèse's novices reported these words (cf. *Test*, 250).

15. *LT* 197 in *GC II*, 999.

16. Ibid.

17. Ibid.

to leave us more frustrated. She shares with Marie the radical assurance that brought Thérèse herself deep joy:

> Your little Thérèse...is weak and very weak, and everyday she has a new experience of this weakness, but, Marie, Jesus is pleased to teach her, as He did Saint Paul, the science of rejoicing in her infirmities. This is a great grace, and I beg Jesus to teach it to you, for peace and quiet of heart are to be found there only.[18]

When we carefully examine the passages in Thérèse's writings that are directly related to confidence, it is remarkable how many times the context is precisely the recognition and acceptance of one's weakness. Paradoxically, what for most of us usually gives rise to disparagement was for her a very privileged source of *joyous assurance*. What for us is so often a stumbling block she actually found to be a stepping stone. Likening herself to a reed, whose frailty redounds to its own advantage—readily bending in a storm rather than breaking—she could say that "its weakness gives rise to all its confidence."[19] Amazingly, she explicitly names this impotence as the specific springboard of her self-giving: "It is my weakness that gives me the boldness of offering myself."[20] Indeed, this frailty is the first characteristic she chooses to give to her little bird, whose joy is to go on gazing at the divine sun, its confidence undiminished by the darkness.

When we look at the influence Saint Thérèse exercised in the years immediately following her death, it is precisely here that we can discern her most dramatic impact. This is all the more astonishing given the remnants of Jansenism still present in the French Church at the turn of the nineteenth century, to which her teaching sounded the final death knell. The Jansenist movement—a gross distortion of the Gospel—had turned the Christian life into a cauldron of cross-examination, a joyless treadmill governed by

---

18. *LT* 109 in *GC I*, 641.
19. *LT* 55 in ibid., 442.
20. *SS*, 195.

fear and grim-faced suspicion. The knitting of eyebrows and flaring of nostrils that it encouraged in the struggle to rid oneself of all trace of imperfection made for much spiritual high blood pressure! Thérèse relieves the tension in this pressure cooker approach to growing in holiness, letting the steam out of the struggle. She invites us to shed such anxiety with regard to our spiritual progress, to let go of our white-knuckled fear of making mistakes, in a way that would have scandalized the Jansenists. She sensed that in this anxiety and fear there was too much introspection, too much self-preoccupation, which is the enemy of any real progress on the spiritual path. "I try to be no longer occupied with myself in anything, and I abandon myself to what Jesus sees fit to do in my soul...."[21]

"Progress," "success," and "achievement" are ideas as foreign to Thérèse as they are a far cry from the Gospels themselves—they do not appear in her dictionary of discipleship. Such concepts are liable to make an idol of the journey of faith itself—a favorite booby trap of the evil one designed specifically for religious professionals! Thérèse dares to dismantle the traditional terminology associated with the way of perfection, standing the accustomed imagery on its head. To one who was being intimidated by thinking of the dizzy heights that had to be conquered in the spiritual life, Thérèse replied:

> I see clearly that you are mistaking the road, and that you will never arrive at the end of your journey. You want to climb the mountain whereas God wishes you to descend it. He is waiting for you in the fruitful valley of humility.[22]

Thérèse's privileged place of meeting the Lord is the holy ground of humility. Jesus waits for us in our weaknesses. He makes a rendezvous of the very things we run away from: failure, disappoint-

---

21. *LT* 247 in *GC II*, 1134.
22. *CR* in *HA*, 229.

ment, inadequacy, and even boredom. Thérèse faces us with the real possibility of making friends with that terrible ennui which can afflict us at times in our discipleship, seizing an opening for growth even in those occasions when we feel we cannot cope with the weight of our Christian responsibilities. "What a grace when, in the morning, we feel no courage, no strength to practice virtue."[23] For Thérèse such occasions were a *kairos*—a time of graced opportunity—announcing the in-breaking of God's own power, precisely because we are unable any longer to hide behind our own competence and self-sufficiency. Indeed, this is where the most significant growth often takes place for us in our following of the Lord. Exploiting the potential of such privileged moments, Thérèse called them "dipping into diamonds."

We see her huge influence at work in the writings of a fellow Frenchwoman and Carmelite contemporary, Elizabeth of the Trinity. She was among the first to have been struck by Thérèse's *Story of a Soul*. In a series of encouraging letters, Elizabeth wrote to someone deeply dismayed by the circumstances in which she found herself, we sense Thérèse's influence at work in the advice Elizabeth gives. She is insistent, first of all, that this is an opportunity to be embraced, not an obstacle to be side stepped. The crisis is essentially one of confidence. Borrowing an image from Thérèse's autobiography, Elizabeth tries to diagnose the dynamics of this situation: it will either strike fear, which will lead to self-defense and consequently to a withdrawal into oneself, or it can inspire surrender and lead to a "launching out on the waves of confidence and love," therefore fastening our focus more completely on God. It is on this flood tide of trust that she would have her friend set sail. In lines that Thérèse herself could have written, Elizabeth makes this invitation:

> Think that the divine artist is using a chisel to make his work more beautiful, and remain at peace beneath the hand that is

---

23. *LT* 65 in *GC I*, 467.

working on you.... [Saint Paul] felt his infirmity and complained about it to God, who answered: "My grace is enough for you, for power is made perfect in weakness."[24]

In this letter, Elizabeth explicitly names Thérèse as the patron saint of such situations, encouraging the person to whom she's writing to claim her intercession. Elizabeth clearly sensed that Thérèse had understood the *joyous assurance* of Saint Paul when faced with such thorns in the flesh (cf. 2 Cor 12:7) and could communicate and even evoke it in others. Both Thérèse and Elizabeth testify to the fact that the situations in which we feel most vulnerable can be the very means by which to intensify our trust: "The more you feel your weakness, the more your confidence must grow...."[25] With the authority of the Apostle, they teach us to make of our liabilities our greatest allies.

Thérèse shows here that the confidence we are discovering as her supreme characteristic is not to be equated with a crude notion of self-confidence. She is not in the business of bolstering the ego or making us feel good about ourselves. Her confidence finds its center of gravity in God alone. One can't help but feel that she would have been at odds with our "I'm okay" culture. For Thérèse this would mean selling ourselves short of the full scale of liberation made possible by Jesus. Instead, she would be the first to admit, "I'm *not* okay," only to add joyfully, "but that's okay!" Like an electric shock, her daring language stops us in our tracks:

> If you are willing to bear serenely the trial of being displeasing to yourself, you will be to me a pleasant place of shelter.[26]

---

24. Elizabeth of the Trinity, *The Complete Works, Volume II, Letters from Carmel* (trans. Anne Englund Nash), Institute of Carmelite Studies, Washington, 1995, 230.

25. Elizabeth of the Trinity, *LT* 324 in ibid., 347.

26. *LT* CLXXXII in *CL,* 303. A psychotherapist, M. Scott Peck, refers to this passage in *People of the Lie: The Hope for Healing Human Evil,* Arrow, London, 1990, 11. Thérèse has been claimed as patron saint of psychotherapists.

These words are found in a Christmas note to her sister Céline, which Thérèse had written as a letter addressed from the Virgin Mary. In it Mary reminds Céline how, with Joseph, she had searched in vain among the inns of Bethlehem to find a place to have her child. She assures Céline that, if she can accept the impoverished state she finds herself in, much like the poverty of the stable that sufficed for Jesus on that first Christmas, she will make a fitting place for Jesus to be born anew. The peace with which she is able to acknowledge and accept her inadequacy will prove to be an irresistible invitation, indeed the best welcome Jesus could wish for. We know that at this time Céline, with her impetuosity, was dealing with a reputation in the Carmel as one prone to outbursts of temper. It seems Thérèse was not simply counseling her sister to swallow her pride, but was making her realize the advantageous nature of this weakness as a highway toward the humility in which Christ has always found his home.

Befriending our frailty and failure, which Thérèse encourages, goes against the grain. It is a lesson that we are forced to grasp again and again through our setbacks and disappointments. The desire to be in control and to want to have something to show for ourselves is a reflex that takes a lifetime to unlearn. We fight all the way to win some shreds of our own righteousness, foraying endlessly in a futile search for our own salvation; and on each occasion defeat delivers a blow and a blessing. But sometimes our evasion of weakness is well disguised. Thérèse tracks down the subtler ways the ego tries to retain control and snatch trophies for itself. Her little way puts us on a collision course with our clambering to possess even spiritual riches. She dares us to relinquish our hold on our spiritual reputation, image, or accomplishment, and to embrace the situations that wrest these from us. Hers is the way of dispossession that leaves us utterly destitute, with nothing to show for ourselves: "In the evening of this life, I shall appear before You with

empty hands."[27] Knowing that empty hands meant they could be
open to receive all that God in his graciousness would freely give,
Thérèse faced this prospect, not with fearful dread but with *joyous
assurance.* Here is the spirit of Mary whose nothingness magnified
the Lord, whose helplessness was the hinge of her utter dependen-
cy upon grace, and whose emptiness was the open door for God's
gracious entry into the world. Thérèse's testimony reverberates
with this same jubilant trust. With a torrent of gratitude welling
up from within, she sings a *magnificat* of her own:

> Almighty God has done great things in me, and the greatest of all
> is to make me conscious of my own littleness, my own incapa-
> city.[28]

---

27. *SS*, 277.
28. *AS*, 251.

~ 6 ~

The Humble Boldness
of Saint Thérèse

I don't hasten to the first place but to the last; rather than advance
like the Pharisee, I repeat, filled with confidence, the publican's
humble prayer. Most of all I imitate the conduct of Magdalene; her
astonishing or rather her loving audacity which charms the Heart
of Jesus also attracts my own.[1]

$\mathcal{P}$ERHAPS THE MOST pernicious source of discouragement in the
life of Christian discipleship, and one which can so sadly and seriously undermine our confidence, is the consciousness of sin. We
need to discover that particular aspect of evangelical assurance that
relates directly to God's forgiveness—"*humble boldness.*" Here Saint
Thérèse astonishes us with still more good news. Hers is the
unhesitating conviction echoing an insight of Julian of Norwich
centuries before—that when surrendered to God's mercy, even sin
itself shall be a glory.

Mary Magdalene best symbolized for Thérèse the audacious
attitude that the Lord allows the sinner to assume before him. Her
conduct is an icon of the confidence he encourages us to adopt in

_____

1. *SS,* 258–9.

his presence. In reflecting upon the Magdalene, Thérèse had three Gospel texts in mind—Luke 7:36–50, Mark 14:3–9, and John 12:1–8—all of which were captured and combined as a single episode in her imagination.[2] Following the popular notion of her day, Thérèse felt that Mary Magdalene was, for her, the central character in all of these texts. In Thérèse's reflections certain elements exercised a profound appeal. Like her spiritual father John of the Cross, she was captivated by the "bold and daring"[3] love that drove this sinner through the doors of the house where Jesus was dining, compelling her to anoint his feet with such selflessness.

First of all, Thérèse is entranced by her entrance! "When I see Magdalene walking up before the many guests..."[4]—the gate-crashing Mary! We may balk at this brazen breach of etiquette, which offers neither apology nor excuse. But Thérèse is transfixed by such astounding behavior, by the fact that this woman is clearly not cowed by the company around her, and that there is not a shred of self-consciousness in her intrusion. In this outrageously daring advance, Thérèse sees the conduct of a sinner supremely confident of her reception. Mary's breaking down the doors of the Law—symbolized by the house of the Pharisee—which kept her outside, denying her access to God's mercy, demonstrates for us the bold approach now possible with the Gospel. Being the "talk of the town" neither intimidates nor inhibits her. Making a beeline for the place where Jesus is sitting, unbowed by the daggered looks and the embarrassment she is causing, she recalls for us that text from the Letter to the Hebrews about "approach[ing] the throne of grace with boldness." Breaking down barriers is underlined by the physical intimacy the Magdalene displays. It is an almost intolera-

---

2. Editor's note: This was common in nineteenth-century spiritual writings, although current scriptural exegesis avoids this juxtaposition.

3. Cf. John of the Cross, *Dark Night of the Soul,* II, 13.9. (trans. E. Allison Peers), Burns & Oates, London, 1976, 138.

4. *LT* 247 in *GC II,* 1133.

ble intimacy, which, to the scandalized Simon's indignation, Jesus does not discourage. This prostitute's shameless presumption outrages all those present, except one. Thérèse understood that Mary's "loving audacity" is precisely what charms "the Heart of Jesus." For Thérèse, Mary almost instinctively knows that "this Heart of love was not only disposed to pardon her but to lavish on her the blessings of His divine intimacy."[5]

Significantly, these words are from a letter to her beloved Bellière, who seems to have had particular difficulties with regard to his acknowledgment and acceptance of the mercy of God. He appears to have been singularly lacking in confidence in this area. Thérèse's correspondence with him consistently returns to this same theme. Bellière himself puts his finger on the problem when he writes:

> What holds me back at times is not Jesus but myself. I am ashamed of myself, and, instead of throwing myself into the arms of this Friend, I hardly dare drag myself to His feet. Often a first inspiration draws me into His arms, but I stop suddenly at the sight of my wretchedness, and I do not dare. Am I wrong?[6]

Bellière does not dare. This is where he is stymied. Instead of being fixed on the place where Jesus is sitting, the throne of mercy, his gaze is focused on himself. He is paralyzed by the pressure of his own self-reproach. How readily we may identify with these sentiments. We have all experienced the same deadlock. Disgusted at the sight of our sinfulness, we hesitate and hold back, forestalling God's forgiveness and effectively standing in the way of our own salvation. Bellière recognized that this was itself one of the most fatal forms of pride. Faced with these symptoms, the medicine Thérèse prescribed is Mary Magdalene. Her *humble boldness* is the most effective antidote to this debilitating condition. In Thérèse's

---

5. Ibid.
6. *LC* 191 in ibid., 1158.

reply to Bellière, she begs her spiritual brother to "follow that 'first impulse'"[7] that he says he often felt. The word she uses here is one we have already met—*élan.* It is the word Pauline used to describe her sister's confidence. Thérèse herself uses this word to define Christian prayer as "a surge of the heart."[8] It is the impulse of love that led Mary to the feet of the Lord. Thérèse wants to teach us that, far from being affronted by such an impulsion, Jesus is actually "thrilled with joy"[9] at those who are bold enough to launch themselves into his arms in this way.

The image of leaping into the arms of one's judge comes through again and again in the teaching of Thérèse. She tells a parable of her own with the explicit intention of showing "how much Jesus loves even imperfect souls who confide in Him."[10] She asks us to imagine two disobedient children, who deserve to be reprimanded by their father. The first runs away in fear, while the other chooses to throw himself into his father's arms, openly protesting his guilt and demanding a kiss as punishment! What parent could resist such "filial confidence"[11] shown by one's child? In this parable Thérèse employs an arresting phrase to describe the child's behavior toward his father. She calls it "taking him by the heart."[12] This seems to have been a favorite expression of hers, for we find it again, in a similar context, among her letters to another of her sisters, Léonie:

> Personally, I find perfection quite easy to practice because I have realized that all one has to do is *take Jesus by the heart.*[13]

---

7. *LT* 261 in ibid., 1164.

8. *CCC,* 2558. The French is *"un élan du coeur."* Clarke's translation has "an aspiration of the heart," *SS,* 242. Knox puts it more lyrically: "a launching out of the heart toward God." *AS,* 289.

9. *LT* 261 in *GC II,* 1165.

10. *LT* 258 in ibid., 1153.

11. Ibid.

12. Ibid., "he is prepared to pardon him always, if his son takes him by his heart."

13. *LT* CLXXI in *CL* 275. Thérèse underlines this expression.

Of all the members of the Martin household, Léonie was the most difficult. It seems she caused her family the greatest grief. She was certainly the one most familiar with failure, having tried to follow her religious vocation four times before she finally persevered. In one of her letters, Léonie expresses a desire to be free from certain scruples that she senses are paralyzing her and preventing her from moving forward on the spiritual path. Much like Bellière, she senses that here she is her own worst enemy: "always drawn in upon myself, I am terribly harmed by this and held back...."[14] In Thérèse's reply, she effectively adapts the above-mentioned parable to illustrate precisely what she thinks should be her sister's strategy. We too might do well to follow Therese's advice when we find ourselves in such a stalemate:

> Consider a small child who has displeased his mother, by flying into a rage or perhaps disobeying her; if he sulks in a corner and screams in fear of punishment, his mother will certainly not forgive his fault; but if he comes to her with his little arms outstretched, smiling and saying: "Kiss me, I *won't do it again*," surely his mother will immediately press him tenderly to her heart, forgetting all that he has done.... Of course she knows quite well that her dear little boy *will do it again* at the first opportunity but that does not matter, if he takes her *by the heart,* he will never be punished.[15]

Thérèse is encouraging her sister to exhibit the winning confidence of a child who openly confesses his or her faults in contrast to one who is fearful and takes off to hide in a corner and wallow in misery. Such a haunting image is one that since Adam has been associated with sin. The effect of our first disobedience was to make us want to hide (cf. Gen 3:8). The trees in the garden, behind which Adam and Eve crouched in hiding, graphically represent the barriers erected by sin's rebellion. Like the veil of Moses and the masks

---

14. *LC* 164 in *GC II*, 964.
15. *LT* CLXXI in *CL*, 275.

of the Pharisees, the fig leaves of our first parents are another metaphor of the situation that *parrhesia* opposes and overturns. In Christ we can stand naked once more before the face of God. Thomas Merton has specifically seen *parrhesia* in these terms. For him it was the "freedom of speech" we enjoyed with God before the fall. It was part of "paradise lost," which has been regained with our redemption. But this is not a simple restoration. Mercy makes possible something still more wonderful:

> *Parrhesia* is a far more marvelous thing in men who are sinners, who are forced to recognize themselves as burdened with guilt, men who have offended God and fled from the sight of Him because they preferred their own illusions to His truth...when the Lord comes into the world as a Savior, the men with whom He seeks to talk familiarly, because He loves them and wants to make them His friends, are precisely the sinners.[16]

The mystery Merton touches here is that in the aftermath of sin and the shame that it has spawned, *parrhesia* is no longer simply original innocence, but something nobler still. It is a shamelessness that now has to run the gauntlet of the voices it once gave in to. It must outface the jibes of our internal jury with its verdict of "guilty!" It is a confidence that chooses to come out of hiding, to give oneself up to mercy, trusting wildly in the promise of salvation rather than being terrorized by the threat of condemnation. It is the mystery portrayed by the Magdalene in the house of the Pharisee. We meet the same language in the parable of the little bird in which Thérèse makes the identical point. The little bird dares to raise its wings, wet with imperfection, to the sun's healing rays rather than "going and hiding away in a corner, to weep over its misery."[17]

In Thérèse's last conversations we find an extension of this same language and imagery. After being shown a picture of our Lord

---

16. Thomas Merton, *The New Man,* Burns & Oates, London, 1962, 67.
17. *SS,* 198.

with two children, one standing at his feet kissing his hand in a respectful way, the other smaller child sitting in his lap, Thérèse remarked, "I'm this very little one who has climbed up on His lap, who is lifting his little head and is caressing Jesus without any fear."[18] All the elements pertaining to the child, which Thérèse reads into the picture, are expressive of the child's confidence, not least of which is the lifting of the child's head to meet the Lord's gaze. We think of the raised head of Jesus at prayer in the *Catechism* icon, and the open elevation exhibited also by the little bird. How often as children, and even still as adults, we avoid making eye contact because of what we fear we may see in the other person's face— rejection, anger, disapproval, disappointment. Thérèse is the child assured that she will see none of these things in the eyes of her Lord, and so she is not afraid to lift her little head and look him straight in the eye.

Thérèse's characteristic attitude is captured for us by an actual incident from her own childhood that her mother recounted. One morning, when Thérèse was five years old, her mother went over to kiss her while she was lying in her bed, still ostensibly asleep. But Thérèse, who had only been pretending to sleep, hid under the blankets like a spoiled child. Her mother left unamused to go downstairs. She describes how little Thérèse followed her minutes later into the kitchen:

> "Mamma," she said, throwing herself at my knees, "Mamma, I was naughty, pardon me!" Pardon was quickly granted. I took my cherub in my arms, pressing her to my heart and covering her with kisses.[19]

We will acknowledge again in the following chapter how deeply Thérèse's childhood, and particularly her relationship with her parents, informed her spirituality. Can we not infer from the incident

---

18. *CJ* 5.7.3 in *Conv*, 74.
19. Extract from Mme. Martin to Pauline dated February 13, 1877, in *GC II*, 1231.

above that the first person to incarnate the mercy of the Lord for Thérèse was her mother? Her arms were the first to make real his merciful embrace. At the very least, being so "well received"[20] on that occasion must have given Thérèse a clue as to the reception she might expect to receive likewise from the Lord.

When asked about the essence of the particular path to holiness she had taken and what it was that she wanted to continue to teach people after her death, Thérèse replied, adapting the startling expression that she felt summed up her strategy:

> ...it's the way of spiritual childhood, it's the way of confidence and total abandon...*to take Him by caresses;* this is the way I've taken Him, and it's for this that I shall be so well received.[21]

The words "well received" lead us into another dimension of confidence in God's mercy. We have seen how in some of the New Testament texts *parrhesia* is a disposition specifically applied to the way the Christian can confidently face the coming of the Lord. This is an aspect, highlighted in Thérèse's teaching, that we find present again in the writings of her fellow Carmelite and kindred spirit, Elizabeth of the Trinity. Hans Urs von Balthasar has pointed to both women as magnificent exemplars of this profoundly biblical disposition. He sees their joint contribution to the Church as reclaiming and rejuvenating such characteristically Christian confidence regarding the last judgment and as encouraging this attitude in us all:

> Both Thérèse and Elizabeth are filled with the New Testament Johannine and Pauline concept of "confidence" (*parrhesia*) in the face of the Day of Judgment. And their confidence does not rest solely on personal election but is a disposition they have been given for the sake of demonstrating it to others.[22]

---

20. Ibid.

21. From a conversation with Pauline in *Conv,* 257. My italics.

22. Hans Urs von Balthasar, *Two Sisters in the Spirit: Thérèse of Lisieux and Elizabeth of the Trinity,* Ignatius Press, San Francisco, 1992, 416.

In her correspondence with Adolphe Roulland, Thérèse expounds on this particular aspect of evangelical assurance. He had written to her from the missions in China, where death was an ever-present reality. Roulland had expressed the fear that if killed, he would not be worthy to enter heaven immediately, and so would need her prayers to draw him out of purgatory. Thérèse cajoles him for his lack of confidence. On one level she knows how pure we need to be to appear in the presence of God. But at the same time she accepts that no one, except the Virgin Mary, has ever been pure enough. The fundamental dispositions of our life are what count. Our love is what matters most.[23] To suggest that the love to which this missionary's life bears witness will not be rewarded is to grossly underestimate not only the mercy but also the very justice of God. "How would He allow Himself to be overcome in generosity?" Whatever may be lacking in terms of our human weakness will, in the mysterious designs of his mercy, be made good "at the moment of appearing before God." Therefore she concludes:

> What have we to fear? ...my way is all confidence and love. I do not understand souls who fear a Friend so tender.[24]

Thérèse will not allow sin to sap her unbreakable and unshakable trust in the immeasurable depths of God's mercy. To those who might be tempted to suggest that the reason for this was because she was not herself conscious of having committed any serious offenses, she says, "Mortal sin wouldn't withdraw my confidence from me."[25] For her, there simply could be no comparison between our sins and his mercy:

---

23. Cf. a conversation with Céline in *Conv,* 262: "...it is love alone that counts." Here she seems to be echoing the teaching of Saint John of the Cross, "at the evening of life, you will be examined in love." *Collected Works of Saint John of the Cross,* op. cit., "Sayings of Light and Love," 57, 672.

24. *LT* 226 in *GC II,* 1093.

25. *CJ* 20.7.3 in *Conv,* 104.

> If I had committed all possible crimes, I would always have the
> same confidence; I feel that this whole multitude of offenses would
> be like a drop of water thrown into a fiery furnace.[26]

The word she uses here is *"jeter"* which draws on the same root as
the English word "jettison." In the name of Jesus, Thérèse dares us
to jettison our sin. She uses the same word to describe not only how
we should throw our sins "with entire filial confidence" into the
devouring flames of the fire of God's love, but also how boldly we
should throw ourselves into the very arms of our judge.

Even this does not capture completely the full extent of how
parrhesia affected Thérèse's attitude toward sin. She believed that
the faults she brought so confidently to the throne of mercy actually redounded to her advantage. In some mysterious way, repentance
made them no longer a stumbling block but, in fact, a stepping
stone. Even our sin is conscripted into the service of our salvation!
She is able to affirm, with all the authority of her own experience
as a sinner, that there is nothing grace cannot make use of:

> I know this as reality:
> The good, the bad in me—the whole,
> Love's Power draws profit from....[27]

In a note to her mother superior, penned after an incident in which
Thérèse had been clearly irritated, we find these audacious sentiments, "Ah, the good it does me for having been bad!"[28] The life
story of little Thérèse confidently testifies to the fact that for those
who love God, all things work out for our benefit (cf. Rom 8:28)—
"even her faults...stood her in good stead to make her grow in perfection."[29] Thérèse is the most eloquent evidence of the way that
the tragedy of sin can actually usher in the triumph of grace. She

---

26. *CJ* 11.7.6 in ibid., 89.
27. *PN* 30, 3 in *Poems*.
28. *LT* 230 in *GC II*, 1100.
29. *SS*, 25.

has sounded the depths of the Pauline doctrine that "where sin increased, grace abounded all the more" (Rom 5:20). In a similar way, Julian of Norwich was shown that sin is no shame but in fact a glory. In her revelations, Julian saw as a fallacy the equation of our falling with any failure of God's love for us. On the contrary, she felt able to affirm that

> we need to fall, and we need to see it; for if we did not fall, we should not know how feeble and how wretched we are in ourselves, nor, too, should we know so completely the wonderful love of our Creator.[30]

Echoing the Easter liturgy's audacious cry—"*O felix culpa!*"—these women would have us discover, and fully exploit, the happy fault our sin can become when surrendered to God's mercy. For Julian, as for Thérèse, it is Mary Magdalene who is the evangelist of this merciful love by which "the mark of sin is turned to honor."[31]

Let us return to this *humble boldness* of the Magdalene, to Thérèse's poetry, and to the text of Saint John in which we have seen *parrhesia* appear alongside the statement that "perfect love casts out fear" (1 Jn 4:18). In what has been acknowledged as Thérèse's finest poem, *Vivre d'Amour,* we find this conviction:

> Living by Love means banishing all fear—
> All glancing-back to faults of earlier day:
> Of my past sins I see no imprint here,
> Love in a trice has burnt them all away![32]

Thérèse sent this poem to Bellière. It meant so much to him that he learned it by heart, so that it could become a part of the living fabric of his daily prayer. He would tell her how precious it was to him and how "in it one breathes in a divine breath making one pure

---

30. Julian of Norwich, *Showings* (trans. Edmund Colledge, O.S.A. and James Walsh, S.J.), *Classics of Western Spirituality,* Paulist Press, New Jersey, 1978, 300.
31. Ibid., 243.
32. *PN* 17, 6 in *Poems.*

and strong...this canticle of love will always accompany me."[33] The poem contains many of the central themes we have already explored—the "heart to heart" and intimate eye contact with the Lord that for her was prayer, the weakness in which she encourages us to rejoice, and the fearlessness that is the touchstone of perfect love. But present also is the *humble boldness* that believes repentance is the amazing grace bringing with it not just pardon but also the privilege of praising him "for evermore."[34]

Thérèse's instinct here is one we find elsewhere in Christian tradition, notably in the wisdom of Bernard of Clairvaux. His lyrical writings proliferate in this profligate mercy of our God. Among his sermons on the Song of Songs, we find a passage laden with the language of *parrhesia*. With regard to the soul bowed down under the weight of its sinfulness, he writes:

> It is my teaching that such a soul...will find a source of boldness so that it may desire marriage with the Word, not fearing to enter into a treaty of friendship with God, nor being timid about taking up the yoke of love.... For what cannot be safely dared when the soul sees itself as his excellent image...?[35]

Here Bernard senses that the key to unlocking the prison in which we languish because of sin is always and only love. This is the supreme reality named by the Lord in the Gospel scene with which we began: "Her sins, which were many, have been forgiven; hence she has shown great love" (Lk 7:47). Thérèse also stakes everything on this scriptural instinct. In the same letter to Bellière with which we began this chapter, she describes how understanding the love of Jesus, as the Magdalene had done, was what had driven every trace of fear from her heart. Toward the end of *Vivre d'Amour*, Thérèse

---

33. *LC* 174 in *GC II,* 1056.
34. *PN* 17, 11, in *Poems.*
35. Sermon 83, 1, translation by Michael Casey in *Athirst for God: Spiritual Desire in Bernard of Clairvaux's Sermons of the Song of Songs,* Cistercian Publications, Kalamazoo, Michigan, 1988, 169.

chooses Mary Magdalene as the perfect model of this "living by love":

> Living by Love—it's like the Magdalene
> Bathing, with tears and precious perfumes there
> Your feet divine, with joyous kiss, and seen
> Wiping them gently with her flowing hair....[36]

The poem continues by focusing on the breaking of the alabaster jar of ointment, an image that seems to capture the violence of love's conversion. Thérèse uses it to express particularly how in losing, one actually gains. This is a wisdom as central to her spirituality as it is to the whole Gospel.[37] She had already used this image in a letter to Céline, in which she wrote of God's ludicrous love in Jesus that seeks out sinners "in order to make them His friends, His intimates, His *equals*."[38] Thérèse goes on in the letter to speak directly of the episode at the house of the Pharisee; underlining the words "breaking the jar," she concludes, "What does it matter if our *vessels* be broken...."[39] This metaphor is also at work in a note written, significantly, on the Feast of Saint Mary Magdalene, in which Thérèse accepts, and indeed asks, to be broken on behalf of sinners, securing by this sacrifice the release of the saving perfume of pardon and forgiveness upon the world.[40] The same striking image appears in another poem written just three years later by Oscar Wilde. Inspired by the same Gospel passage, behind the bars not of Carmel but of Reading Gaol, Wilde composed the following lines, which powerfully proclaim the radical grace of repentance and describe the shattering of the heart accompanying the gift of salvation:

---

36. *PN* 17, 12 in *Poems.*
37. On Cèline's coat of arms she wrote the motto "who loses wins [*Qui perd gagne*]." *LT* 183 in *GC II,* 932.
38. *LT* 169 in *GC II,* 882. Thérèse underlined the word "equals."
39. Ibid., 883.
40. *LT* 259 in ibid., 1159–60.

And every human heart that breaks,
  In prison-cell or yard,
Is as that broken box that gave
  Its treasure to the Lord,
And filled the unclean leper's house
  With the scent of costliest nard.

Ah! happy they whose hearts can break
  And peace of pardon win!
How else may man make straight his plan
  And cleanse his soul from Sin?
How else but through a broken heart
  May Lord Christ enter in?[41]

---

41. Oscar Wilde, "The Ballad of Reading Gaol," V.

~ 7 ~

Saint Thérèse and Her Certainty of Being Loved

$\mathcal{T}$HE *CATECHISM'S* final description for *parrhesia* captures a further aspect of the fundamental disposition of a Christian disciple— and one under particular threat in the present climate in which we live—*"the certainty of being loved."* We have already become aware of the dimension of "spiritual childhood" in the doctrine of Saint Thérèse. Here we shall delve still more deeply into this aspect of her teaching. She helps us to understand why Jesus set a child in front of the disciples to convey most convincingly what he was trying to say to them about the Kingdom (cf. Mt 18:1–5). Moreover, in Thérèse herself we are actually confronted with such a child, whom God has set before the Church of our time to show how lavishly he loves us.

As we have already hinted, the origins of her way of "spiritual childhood" are to be found in the atmosphere of her own home— Les Buissonnets. At the beginning of her autobiography, she recalls the abundant blessing of an upbringing in which she was surrounded by affection. By her own admission, Thérèse, as the youngest, was "the most loved,"[1] among her sisters. This is corroborated by

---

1. *SS*, 93.

those who knew the Martin family. Much can be gathered from the many affectionate nicknames she was given—"Benjamin," "little Pearl," and "Queen of my heart." The latter was the term of endearment that her father preferred. Theirs was clearly a unique relationship. He played a leading role in the story of her soul. Thérèse recalls in vivid detail how, after her mother's death when Thérèse was only four years old, her father's affection for her now "seemed to be enriched...with a truly maternal love."[2] The early pages of her autobiography are filled with memories of the walks they took together, the games they played, the times he carried her on his shoulders. Memories of details, like the expression on his face in church or when they said their prayers at bedtime, made a deep impression on her. "I cannot say how much I loved Papa; everything in him caused me to admire him."[3] But still more important was the primacy and precedence of his love for her. Thérèse filled her father's horizons. She knew that she was loved.

Given all this, she was in a privileged position to relate readily to God as Jesus encourages us in the Gospels—and with quite a head start on most of us! For Thérèse there was clearly an interplay between the relationship she enjoyed with her earthly father and the one she could enjoy with her Heavenly Father. If Pauline gave "visibility" to Jesus, then her father gave "tangibility" to God's love for her. In her letters to him from Carmel she could write, "When I think of you, dear little Father, I naturally think of God."[4]

Yet even this doesn't prepare us for the jolt of hearing Thérèse refer to God as *"Papa le bon Dieu"*[5] which breaks with traditional nomenclature, derailing our routine ways of respecting the majesty of God. We are ambushed by such arresting intimacy! Here is all the breathtaking familiarity of Jesus' own "Abba! Father!"—but in her

---

2. *SS*, 35.
3. Ibid., 48.
4. *LT* 58 in *GC I*, 452.
5. *CJ* 5.6.4 in *OC*, 1009.

own mother tongue. Céline recalls how once, during Thérèse's last days when she referred to God in this way, everyone around her laughed. Then with deep emotion Thérèse insisted, "Oh! yes, He is indeed my 'Papa' and how sweet it is for me to call Him by this name."[6] This "nickname," at once filled with such innocence and impudence, expressed for Thérèse the certain trust that she was loved by God in the same unconditional way she associated with her parents' love at Les Buissonnets. Hans Urs von Balthasar has been persuaded of how profoundly one influenced and informed the other:

> Everything Thérèse achieves at the supernatural level is rooted in something she has experienced at the natural level. Nothing moved her more, perhaps, than the experience of being loved by her father and mother.[7]

The congruity is further underlined in her description of the day she made her religious profession. Her father was unable to be at the ceremony because of illness. This seems only to have strengthened for Thérèse the staggering implications of the first line of the Lord's Prayer. It struck her with full force, in a way reminiscent of Francis of Assisi returning his clothes to his father in the public square in Assisi. On that occasion Francis had remarked how, for the first time in his life, he felt really free to say, "Our Father who art in heaven." Of this similar milestone in her own life, Thérèse recalls:

> On the day of my wedding I was really an orphan, no longer having a Father on this earth and being able to look to heaven with confidence, saying in all truth: "Our *Father* who art in Heaven...."[8]

This wrenching incident was reinforced by the extended separation caused by Monsieur Martin's mental illness. The final severing came with his death five years later. In a letter to Céline, Thérèse

---

6. Cf. *Conseils et Souvenirs* published by Sister Geneviève and quoted by Jean Lafrance in *My Vocation Is Love: Thérèse of Lisieux,* St. Pauls, Slough, 1990, 118.

7. Hans Urs von Balthasar, op.cit., 25.

8. *SS,* 161. Thérèse underlined the word "Father."

again highlights the significance of these painful events in helping her to enter into the spirit of the Lord's Prayer and cleave more completely to God:

> He took from us the one whom we loved with so much tenderness.... But was it not so that we could truly say "Our Father, who art in heaven"? Oh! how consoling are these words, what infinite horizons they open to our eyes....[9]

Thérèse touches here a taproot of discouragement at the heart of our human experience, which causes the hemorrhaging of trust and confidence: when those from whom we have felt *the certainty of being loved* are taken from us. The distress caused when fragile and finite human love was cut short found a purpose in her life. It led her to the threshold of the infinite horizons of divine love and the certainty that such a love would never be found wanting. Here Thérèse stands as patron saint of those whose confidence has been dented and undermined by disappointment, whether through bereavement, a failed relationship, or one that is faltering through mistrust or fear.

We discovered fearlessness to be an important aspect of the *parrhesia* of the New Testament. For Thérèse, this lack of fear is directly related to a child's *certainty of being loved.* How often, in the context of the image of a child in the arms of a mother or father, we find the expression "without any fear,"[10] almost like a refrain. In a poem about the particular "melody" we hear played in the life and martyrdom of Saint Cecilia, we hit upon these lines:

> *Surrender* (words all fail) /—Divine the melody!
> In that celestial hymn / was love made manifest:
> Such love as *does not fear,* / forgetting all, to be
> Upon the Heart of God / a little child at rest....[11]

---

9. *LT* 127 in *GC II,* 724. Cf. also *LT* 101 in *GC I,* 602, "now we are orphans, but we can say with love: 'Our Father, who art in heaven.'"

10. Cf. *SS,* 188, *LT* 196 in *GC II,* 994, *LT* 263, in ibid., 1173, *CJ* 5.7.3 in *Conv,* 74.

11. *PN* 3, 29–32 in *Poems.* In *OC,* 639 the reference in line 31 to 1 John 4.18 is noted.

Ever since her visit to Rome and to the Catacombs, Thérèse felt a special affection and affinity for Saint Cecilia. In her account of that pilgrimage, she tells us why she had developed such devotion for this young woman and adopted her as a personal patron saint. What attracted her most of all about this martyr was "her *abandonment,* her limitless confidence."[12] Here we come upon another word in Thérèse's vocabulary coupled with "confidence" and pertinent to our subject—in French, "*abandon.*"

Often translated as "abandonment" or "surrender," it emphasizes the absence of inhibition in a child resting secure in its mother's arms, so utterly sure of her love. It is striking to notice just how many times the word "abandon," like the expression "without fear," occurs in direct relation to this imagery.[13] Indeed, for Thérèse abandonment and the absence of fear are opposite sides of the same reality. So many of the elements associated with the concept of *parrhesia,* seem to converge in this primal image of the confidence of a babe-in-arms, who rests secure in the felt knowledge that he or she is cherished.

The image is profoundly scriptural. In her autobiography, Thérèse cites twice a text from the prophet Isaiah, which for her was paramount. She remarks that "never did words more tender and more melodious come to give joy to my soul."[14] She felt she had found what she was looking for in this word of the Lord:

> As a mother caresses her child, so will I comfort you; I will carry you on my breast, and upon my knees I shall caress you (Is 66:13, 12).[15]

---

12. *SS,* 131.

13. Cf. *SS,* 188, *LT* 196 in *GC II,* 994, and *LT* 263 in ibid., 1173, also *LT* 205 in ibid., 1033 and *LT* 226 in ibid., 1094.

14. *SS,* 208.

15. *Manuscript "B"* 1, 42 and 2, 23 in *OC,* 220 and 238. Thérèse adapts the text slightly, reversing the two verses and making the sense more direct. In the second citation she changes the last phrase to "I will dandle you on my knees." The translation here is my own.

Here is an example of how instinctively biblical is the spirituality
of Saint Thérèse of Lisieux with its predilection for the images of
trust found there—the shepherd and his sheep, the hen and her
chicks, the mother and her child. Furthermore, the language at
work strongly echoes the prologue of the Gospel of Saint John,
where Jesus is described as being "close to the Father's heart"
(1:18).[16] It seems to underline the sense that the degree of immediacy with which the Son relates to the Father is also freely available to us. This is emphasized still further when we realize that the
expression used for "close to the Father's heart" is akin to the one
used to describe the way the beloved disciple leaned on Jesus'
breast at the Last Supper (cf. Jn 13:23). In Thérèse, equivalence
clearly exists between her image of a child on its mother's breast
and that of the disciple on his Master's breast. Both images convey
an intimacy, the secrets of which we are all invited to share. She
employs this image powerfully in another poem:

> Recall: as though inebriate, St. John,
> Apostle-Virgin, rested on Your breast.
> Pure tenderness was what he lay upon:
> He knew Your Secrets in that holy rest!
> That Loved Disciple can
>   no jealousy arouse—
> *I* know Your Secrets, too,
>   O Lord! I am Your spouse.
>   My Savior, I'm caressed,
>   I'm lulled, upon the breast
>   Of You, my All.[17]

Two other images appear, and too often not to be significant, in the
cluster of images surrounding this *certainty of being loved.* They are
the storm and the darkness, and "abandonment" is central in both.

---

16. Cf. the French *"sur mon sein* [on my breast]" of the Isaiah text and the *"vers le
sein* [towards / in the breast]" of John's Prologue [*JB* French edition].

17. *PN* 24, 20 in *Poems.*

How many times Thérèse likens her confidence to the fearless trust
of a child cradled in the arms of a parent, or resting on Jesus' breast
in the thick of night or in the midst of a raging storm. Once more *storm*
to her spiritual brother Bellière she writes:

> You must sail the stormy sea of the world with the abandonment
> and the love of a child who knows his Father loves him.[18]

In other places her language explicitly recalls the storm in which
the disciples were caught on the Sea of Galilee—the occasion when
Jesus was in the boat but asleep in the stern. To her correspondents
Thérèse's message in this context is always the same: "Why fear the
storm...we are in the arms of Jesus."[19] Jesus was not intimidated.
Neither would she be. Just as Jesus was fast asleep on the cushion,
she pictures herself in one poem drowsing upon his heart in the
heart of the tempest:

> My Heaven, *always,* in
>   His presence, I shall stay,
> A child—in calling Him
>   the "Father" that He is.
> I do not fear the storm,
>   I'm safe in His embrace;
> I've one rule only—that's:
> "Surrender totally."[20]

This had been an important image for Thérèse even before she
entered Carmel. When she returned home with a heavy heart from
Christmas Midnight Mass the year she had hoped she would be
allowed to enter, Thérèse found in her room a present from her sister Céline. Floating in her washbasin was a little boat her sister had
made. Inside it were figures of the sleeping Jesus and Thérèse at his
side. Written on the sail of the boat were words taken from the

---

18. *LT* 258 in *GC II,* 1152.
19. *LT* 149 in ibid., 826–7. cf. also *LT* 161 in ibid., 851, *LT* 167 in ibid., 872,
LT 171 in ibid., 888–9.
20. *PN* 32, 4 in *Poems.*

Scriptures: "I slept, but my heart was awake" (Song 5:2). But most significant of all was the name of the boat: "*Abandon*"—"Abandonment," "Surrender."

Years later Thérèse's language in a letter to a disconsolate Céline seems to recall this gift. Employing the same image, though with a slight twist that serves to reinforce fearlessness in the face of the storm, Thérèse pictures Céline, with all the trials she is going through, as a little child apparently all alone in a boat lost at sea.[21] Disorientated by the storm, "the only thing she can do is abandon herself and allow her sail to flutter in the wind." Thérèse assures Céline that she is not alone. Jesus is in the boat, but he is asleep. Then Thérèse focuses on the pillow upon which he is sleeping: "it is the heart of a *child*."

It is Céline's own heart. The genius of this curious twist is the realization that, if Jesus has made a cushion of her companionship, Céline will not want to disturb him until he is ready to awaken. She is providing him with rest, which in turn provides her with the assurance that all will be well. Her filial trust in the face of the storm is being drawn from her by the very realization that she is giving him refuge. Allowing us to take on such importance for him swells in us the sense that we are cherished. What confidence this conviction increases! Being treated like this only serves to reinforce *the certainty of being loved.* Let the tempest rage and roar, and the night run its course—she will be as undisturbed as Jesus.

Thérèse conceives of the consolation that Céline is giving to the Lord as hidden from her by the darkness: "He is happy to receive all from her during the *night.*"[22] Night is, especially for children, the place primarily associated with uncertainty and fear. In a note to one of the sisters, Thérèse gently teases, "How naughty to spend one's night in fretting, instead of falling asleep on the Heart of

21. *LT* 144 in *GC II,* 803-5.
22. Ibid., 804. Thérèse has underlined the word "night."

Jesus!"[23] Her advice in the nightmarish darkness is not to complain that one cannot see, but actually to decline the desire to see and to dare to close one's eyes. Her strategy is "not to struggle against the chimeras of the night," but to surrender oneself in the certainty that we are being carried. She counsels us to consent *not* to see; such consent confounds the "empty fear" that she felt unfitting for a little child.

C. Fitzgerald

Thérèse wrote the note to Céline in December 1896. She herself had already been surrounded by darkness for six months. From Easter that year she had found herself "in the midst of the darkest storm."[24] She uses different images to describe this trial of faith. It felt as if an iron curtain had come down between herself and heaven; that she was crawling through an underground tunnel, traveling through a thick fog, or into a black hole. All of these images point to the same stark reality: "Everything has disappeared!"[25] The horror of this Gethsemane would end only with her death. Its disorientation deprived her of all feeling of God's presence. She was despoiled of every support, her only bearings supplied by *the certainty of being loved,* which she would not relinquish, even though it was unfelt. Thérèse borrows the language of John of the Cross, the patron saint of the Dark Night, to describe this paradox lying at the heart of the paschal mystery: "Supported, but with no support!"[26] She faced the onslaught, as Jesus had done in the garden, with a child's cry of abandonment: "Abba! Father!" (cf. Mk 14:36). In this connection, Noel Dermot O'Donohue, a distinguished Carmelite theologian and spiritual writer, draws an authoritative link between the *parrhesia* of the *Catechism* and the witness of Thérèse of Lisieux:

---

23. *LT* 205 in ibid., 1033.

24. *SS,* 190.

25. Ibid., 213.

26. Cf. *PN* 30, in *Poems.* Thérèse bases this poem on one by John of the Cross: *Glosa a lo Divino* cf. *Collected Works,* op. cit., 734–5.

It is through the presence and power of the Spirit that we are given that "freedom of speech," that *parrhesia*, that "boldness" of the little way of Saint Thérèse of Lisieux by which she walked foolishly childish into that very place on the Mount of Olives where the great *pierasmos* of the Lord's Prayer was faced in all its terror and undoing.[27]

How does Thérèse manifest confidence in her own Gethsemane? Where do we see her *parrhesia* in the face of the *pierasmos*—a time of testing and trial—that she describes as "the night of nothingness"?[28] As in the note to Céline, so here her response is: exactly *not* to awaken the sleeping Jesus. It is to meet the trial with yet more trust—a trust she more clearly manifests in actually declining the desire to see. Overtaken by pitch darkness, one's natural reaction is to strain toward some shred of light or to shut one's eyes tight in sheer panic. Thérèse, instead, chooses to close her eyes with a confidence that beggars our comprehension:

> I've had a greater desire not to see God...and to remain in the night of faith, than others have desired to see and understand.[29]

The more deafening the darkness, the more she will push her confidence—to the point of no return. She expresses this unbearable boldness, stretched to such extreme limits, in the words of Job, which had always fascinated her and to which she now allies herself so utterly: "Although he should kill me, I will trust in him" (cf. Job 13:15). This degree of abandonment is possible because, in the face of all the evidence, she refuses to let go of the hope that she is being held in his arms.

Years before, on the occasion of her First Holy Communion, Thérèse had received a prayer card with a poem printed on it. She bears witness to the significance of this poem in her autobiography.

---

27. Noel Dermot O'Donohue, "The Lord's Prayer" in (Ed) Michael Walsh, *Commentary on the Catechism of the Catholic Church,* Geoffrey Chapman, London, 1994, 414.
28. *SS*, 213.
29. *CJ* 11.8.5 in *Conv,* 146.

Its title, "The Little Flower of the Divine Prisoner," reveals the future bearing it would have on her spirituality, but so do its contents. In the poem, Jesus describes the roots this little flower must have, planted as it is in the soil of naked faith:

> For this tender flower I would have as Root
> That trust in Me which never grows weak;
> Infinite hope in My divine Bounty,
> That surrender of the child who knows I love it.[30]

The certainty of being loved makes possible surrender and lack of fear, which are the hallmarks of the little children to whom Christ promises the Kingdom of heaven. These dimensions of Thérèse's doctrine of "spiritual childhood" help to clarify why *parrhesia* has become permanently associated with praying the Lord's Prayer. It is the spirit of those who know they are cherished. It is the perspective of Jesus, who knows his name is "Beloved" (Mk 1:11), and who dares us to say with him, "Father!" Thérèse's message drives home the fact that the characteristic stance of the Christian is quintessentially that of a child; that the fundamental disposition of a disciple of Jesus is that of a son, a daughter. On a visit to Lisieux, Pope John Paul II chose to sum up this saint's chief contribution to the life of the Church as recovering and rejuvenating for the present generation precisely this sense of our spirit of adoption (cf. Rom 8:15). Having spoken explicitly about her "filial trust," he then said:

> Through her life, short and hidden but so rich, [Thérèse] uttered with particular forcefulness, "Abba! Father!" Thanks to her the entire Church has found again the whole simplicity and freshness of this cry, which has its origin and its source in the heart of Christ.[31]

---

30. *GC II,* 1278.

31. Homily of John Paul II in Lisieux, June 1980 quoted in *L'Osservatore Romano,* English edition (June 23, 1980). Used with permission.

·: 8 :·

Under the Rays of the Sun

I see myself as a feeble little bird, with only a light down to cover me; I am not an eagle, yet I have an eagle's *eyes* and an eagle's *heart*, for in spite of my extreme littleness, I dare to gaze upon the divine Sun, the Sun of Love, and my heart feels within it all the eagle's aspirations.[1]

*T*HIS SUBLIME PARABLE appears in Thérèse's autobiography, bringing together each aspect of her fearless trust and boundless confidence. The many strands of Christian *parrhesia* are woven together in this one striking illustration, which Thérèse herself refers to as "the story of my little bird,"[2] and which poignantly depicts her characteristic understanding of living by grace.

The parable was originally part of a letter written to her sister Marie, in response to her request for some reflections during what was surely to be Thérèse's last retreat. Marie's letter is itself revealing and helps to set the scene for the answer she is given.[3] In it she asks to be let into "the secrets of Jesus to Thérèse." Marie wants to

---

1. *LT* CLXXV in *CL,* 284. I have used Sheed's translation when citing from the text of the parable unless otherwise indicated. The complete text can be found in *CL,* 283–287 and *SS,* 198–200.

2. *LT* 197 in *GC II,* 999.

3. *LC* 169 in ibid., 991–2.

be allowed an insight into what she senses is the privileged relationship her godchild shares with the Lord. She desires to love him
in the same way. Significantly, she draws a direct comparison
between the trusting relationship Thérèse enjoys with Jesus and
the one this youngest sister once shared with their father:

> Ah! the little Thérèse...the darling whom Jesus (just as in the past
> her dear little father) holds by the hand...her heavenly Spouse does
> not mislead her anymore than did her father.... He does not let her
> fall.... He rocks her gently on His Heart, He smiles at her aban-
> donment.

Recognizing such radical intimacy in the relationship between Jesus
and Thérèse fueled a desire in her sister for the same holy familiarity. The knowledge that here was someone for whom Jesus was her
"entire fortune" prompted Marie to seek the same prosperity.

Thérèse prefaces her reply by attesting that what follows will
contain, as her sister had requested, her "*little* doctrine."[4] She will
attempt to paint a picture of all that God has graciously revealed to
her, lamenting before she begins the lack of colors in her palette to
express perfectly what she means. Many would contend that, on the
contrary, it is nothing short of a masterpiece. The three sheets of
paper that make up Manuscript "B" are the distillation of her holy
daring. Dated September 8, 1896, they are addressed directly to
Jesus. The first coughings of blood that signaled the onset of her
tuberculosis had occurred in April. Shortly after, her trial of faith
began. She was already in a state of extreme fatigue, as is evident
from the many corrections with which the original manuscript is
covered.

The immediate context of her parable is the gap Thérèse senses between the aspirations she feels in her heart and her ability to
fulfill them. She pictures the great saints as eagles whose wings
carry them soaring into the heights. In contrast, she is just a fledg-

---

4. *SS*, 189.

ling. Nevertheless, she has an eagle's eyes and heart. With her heart she aspires to those same altitudes. With her eyes she "dares" to fix her gaze on the goal of her desires—the divine sun. She lifts her little wings, expressing her will to fly toward the sun. But raising her wings is all she is able to do. Here we have in synthesis her stance before God. It is clearly reminiscent of the icon of Christ at prayer —the raised eyes, the lifted arms, the gaze of faith riveted on God: the posture of *parrhesia.*

Looking heavenward, this little bird's "uncovered eye" expresses unhindered communication. Its eyes are attracted by, and engaged with, the "Divine gaze,"[5] which "from instant to instant" reciprocates that open dialogue. This imagery captures Thérèse's fundamental description of prayer as "a simple glance directed to heaven."[6]

The language here too reflects once again the *straightforward simplicity* of Thérèse's prayer. She feels free to be frank with the Lord. She takes her questions, her quandaries, and her inability to grasp his ways, directly to him, tackling him with them in no uncertain terms. There is no pretense to this prayer—all protocol is dispensed with. Once more she presumes to use the familiar *"tu"* form, and the subject matter is simply what "my heart feels":

> "Are my measureless desires only but a dream, a folly? ...Explain this mystery to me!"[7]

The little bird is well aware of its weakness, which is emphasized both by its "extreme littleness" and by the fact that it still has a fledgling's features. It hasn't yet lost its down, and its feathers have hardly formed. It may raise its wings in an expression of its desire to take flight, but "to fly—that is not in its small power." How does the bird react to its impotence? Not with disparagement, but

---

5. The expression *"Divin regard"* is used three times in this parable.
6. *SS,* 242. Cf. *CCC,* 2558.
7. Ibid., 197.

with "bold surrender."[8] It keeps its eyes trained on the object of its desires. It is not cowed by its incapacity. It harnesses this weakness as the very means to redouble its confidence. It will not be intimidated—"nothing can affright it"—even when the clouds come to hide the sun from its sight. When this happens—as indeed it had at that time in Thérèse's life—"the little bird does not move." Despite everything, it will not change its place. It will not seek to exchange the circumstances in which it finds itself for a situation it might find more tolerable. It stays. Even when the light is taken away, it will remain there staring up at the place where the sun once was; and, paradoxically, this for the little bird is the moment of "perfect joy." Its gaze of faith locked on this invisible light is filled with the *joyous assurance* that beyond the clouds the sun is still shining. Thérèse names this eclipse in which she finds herself stranded as "the hour in which to push my confidence to its uttermost bounds."[9]

The confidence of this fledgling when faced with its "misdeeds" is similarly undiminished. We hear the clear echoes of Thérèse's other parables when she tells us that the little bird,

> Instead of going and hiding away in a corner, to weep over its misery and to die of sorrow, the little bird turns toward its beloved Sun, presenting its wet wings to its beneficent rays.[10]

Its sinful condition, surrendered to the healing rays of God's mercy, is seen here not as a stumbling block but as a stepping stone. Like its weaknesses, its "infidelities" too, when recounted and repented of, actually work to the little bird's advantage. Like the Magdalene, its misdeeds are, in a mysterious way, precisely what occasions and spurs on the "audacity of its total trust." Although it seems presumptuous, this little bird in its *humble boldness* doesn't doubt that

---

8. Ibid., 198. Sheed's translation is "reckless abandon."

9. *HA*, 187.

10. *SS*, 198.

God will draw profit from its sin. Although it seems preposterous, it believes

> that it will acquire in even greater fullness the love of *Him* who came to call not the just but sinners.[11]

Thérèse likewise employs the imagery of the darkness and the storm in this story. Despite being overtaken by the darkness and being battered and buffeted by the storm, the little bird will not withdraw its trust. It will not give up its *certainty of being loved,* even though all evidence seems to point to the contrary. Even when its prayers are left unanswered and the heavens remain indifferent and apparently "deaf to the plaintive chirping of the little creature," still this bird will not yield up its confidence. Even when it does not feel anything any more, including God's own love for which it has ventured everything, it will stay in its place—it accepts "its numbness from the cold." It will not relinquish the reckless trust that it is living "under the rays of the Sun," even though it cannot feel their warmth. Here her parable portrays how profoundly Thérèse had been plunged into the full depths of the paschal mystery. Like her Lord, she outstares the darkness with perfect love.

Thérèse is conscious of the forces of discouragement that threaten to shake her assurance. She pictures them as vultures preying on her vulnerability. She hears the darkness mocking her and telling her that all these thoughts of heaven are simply fantasies, a meaningless mirage that will betray her hope and leave her bereft.[12] She confides to Pauline how she is obsessed by "frightful thoughts" and how the evil one is trying to deceive her.[13] His strategy is to dismantle and demolish her conviction that she is loved, insinuating that this is just a fairy tale: "'Are you certain God loves you? Has He Himself told you so?'"[14]

---

11. Ibid., 199.
12. Ibid., 213.
13. From a conversation with Pauline in *Conv,* 257.
14. *HA,* 205.

Thérèse is not taken in by these tactics. She recognizes what is happening and "she has no fear" of the vulturous voices. She calls on the other eagles to defend her cause and chase off these attacks, leaving her as prey only to the divine eagle, Jesus. She senses that the other eagles, the saints, want to see to what lengths this little bird is prepared to stretch its trust: "...how far I'm going to push my confidence."[15] But in the face of the divine folly, her *filial trust* is without frontiers: "How can my trust have any limits?" The little bird is fully assured that it will fly. It will soar to the loftiest heights, "flying upward to the Sun of Love with the divine Eagle's own wings!" This image underlines for us the fact that for Thérèse, Jesus was everything—her virtue, her sanctity, her prayer. He was her whole reality: "Only Jesus *is:* everything else *is not.*"[16] It was up to him to achieve; it was up to her to surrender. The final lines of this parable definitively name the disposition that gives birth to such abandonment: "entire trust."

After reading these pages, Marie wrote to Thérèse to say how grateful she was to receive them. Ironically, reading those "lines that are not from earth but an echo from the Heart of God"[17] seems to have made her all the more acutely aware that she did not share her sister's sanctity. Thérèse wrote back immediately. There is almost exasperation in her tone:

> How can you ask me if it is possible for you to love the good God as I love Him? ...If you had understood the story of my little bird, you would not ask me such a question.[18]

The whole point of her parable was to trace the profile of a holiness that is open to all. Thérèse's little bird has eagle's aspirations. Those desires reveal the very grace that God wants to give. After all, he

---

15. *CJ* 22.9.3 in *Conv,* 195. These words were recorded just a week before Thérèse's death.

16. *LT* LXXIV in *CL,* 113. Thérèse underlines the words in italics.

17. *LC* 170 in *GC II,* 997.

18. *LT* CLXXVI in *CL,* 288.

put them there in the first place, "and God never gives desires He cannot fulfill..." Marie's question itself shows that she has those same aspirations. Therefore, of course it is possible to love Jesus as Thérèse does. Indeed, the very desire is not only a sign that God has this grace in store for her but that he has, in a real sense, "already given it." Thérèse realizes that she is touching on a tremendous mystery here and that she is straining the limits of human language to the breaking-point. She uses a characteristic phrase, which appears in her writings when she is trying to communicate something crucial and can barely be put into words, "Oh! how I wish I could make you realize what I mean!"[19] It is all the more powerful here because it counters her sister's "I wish I could [be like you]" in Marie's previous letter to Thérèse. It is precisely at this point that she breaks through to what is surely the most magnificent summary not only of this parable but also of the whole of her "little doctrine":

It is trust, and nothing but trust, that must bring us to Love.

The accounts of Thérèse's last days testify to the extremes to which her trust was exposed. They reveal the intense anguish of the final ordeal she was to suffer. The full horror of those last hours is almost unbearable to read. She is exposed to unimaginable desolation—laid waste, despoiled. On September 30, 1897, the day of her death, those around her witnessed the terrible force of the disintegration and discouragement she was facing: "I can't take anymore!...I can't take anymore! ...I am reduced."[20] But they also found themselves face to face with the terrifying force of her *filial trust* and the full extent of her surrender: "I am not sorry for delivering myself up to Love.... Oh! no, I'm not sorry; on the contrary!"[21]

19. Cf. also *LT* 258 in *GC II,* 1152.
20. Reported by Marie in *Conv,* 243.
21. *CJ* 30.9 in ibid., 205.

Conclusion

A Double Share of Her Spirit

The personal charism of some witnesses to God's love for men has been handed on, like "the spirit" of Elijah to Elisha and John the Baptist, so that their followers may have a share in this spirit.[1]

*T*HIS PASSAGE from the *Catechism* recalls the episode in the Old Testament when Elisha, on the occasion of Elijah's ascent into heaven, dared to ask for a share in his master's spirit (cf. 2 Kings 2:1–18). As the time of the prophet Elijah's departure drew near, his servant Elisha never left his master's side, sensing the imminence of their impending separation. When that moment could no longer be delayed, Elijah gave his servant leave to make one final request. In Hebrew tradition, the eldest son stood to inherit a double portion of his father's property (cf. Deut 21:17). In asking for a double share of his master's spirit, Elisha was asking to be recognized as the principal spiritual heir to Elijah's prophetic gifts— a bold request indeed! Elijah ascended in his fiery chariot, but he left behind his mantle as a sign that Elisha's request had been granted. Some icons choose to depict Elisha clinging to Elijah's mantle as he is caught up in the whirlwind of fire, capturing vivid-

---

1. *CCC*, 2684.

ly Elisha's vehement desire that his wish not be ignored and that his master's spirit be passed on to him.

In her autobiography, Thérèse recalls this very episode. Presuming to address the whole communion of saints, and claiming their intercession, she makes a similar appeal: "It is bold, I know; however, I dare to ask you to obtain for me YOUR TWOFOLD LOVE."[2] It is clear from the context that she is asking for a double dose of their love—nothing more and nothing less! Once more we are witnessing here her *parrhesia*—her exorbitant audacity. There is nothing demure about her demands. She makes no apology for the extravagant nature of her request. If Elisha could lodge such an appeal, then why not Thérèse? Some might call it presumption, but she saw it as actually honoring God with her enterprising hope. She taught her novices that they could never have too much confidence in God, and that they should expect everything from him "as a little child expects everything from its father."[3] She was fond of repeating the wisdom of John of the Cross, to which she had wedded herself so faithfully in her own Christian journey: "The soul obtains from God all that it hopes to receive from Him."[4]

As the time for her own departure from this life drew near, those who knew and loved her felt impelled to make a similar request. The sisters around her bedside and those with whom she was in correspondence were asking her, as it were, for a share of her spirit. To one of the sisters distressed at the thought of Thérèse's imminent death, she writes a note in which she uses the image with which we have become so familiar. She likens that sister to a little bird perched upon a branch that is about to break. The branch is clearly Thérèse, on whom this sister has come to rely so heavily. Thérèse encourages her to see that this is the opportunity to take

---

2. *SS*, 196.

3. *CJ* 6.8.8 in *Conv*, 138.

4. John of the Cross, *Dark Night* II, 21.8 in *Collected Works*, op. cit., 380.

flight on the wings of confidence and love to which she had intro-
duced her:

> He alone must be enough for us when it pleases Him to take away
> the branch supporting the little bird! The bird has wings, it is
> made for flying![5]

In similar vein she comforted her sister Céline, who was telling
another sister near Thérèse's bedside that she would not be able to
live without her. Thérèse interrupted her sister, saying, "That's
right; so I'll bring you two wings!"[6]

But nobody exhibits the spirit of Elisha better than her beloved
Bellière. In one of his last letters to Thérèse, he writes, "I believe
and hope and expect from you this *loving confidence* that I still lack
and ardently desire."[7] We sense here the robust determination of an
Elisha not to let his teacher go without leaving behind her mantle.
And clearly from his tone the spirit of his tutor was already rub-
bing off!

As a token of her affection and pledge of her continued advoca-
cy, Thérèse left to her spiritual brother a relic she had kept since her
clothing as a novice: the crucifix Léonie had given her when she was
thirteen years old and that had been blessed by the Pope at that
unforgettable audience. She also gave Bellière the last picture she
had painted. She referred to these as his *"inheritance."*[8] Though
overwhelmed by these gifts, he was in no doubt as to the real legacy she was bequeathing him. It was the little way she had pointed
out. He was already "making a sweet habit of her holy intimacy."[9]
This was the fortune to which he felt he had become an heir. He

---

5. *LT* 250 in *GC II*, 1138

6. From a conversation reported by Céline in *Conv,* 219. Cf. the note which
explains the play on words at work here. Céline has said that she couldn't live without her [*elle*]. Thérèse retorts with her promise to provide her with wings [*ailes*].

7. *LC* 193 in *GC II*, 1171.

8. Cf. *LT* 263 in ibid., 1173–4. Thérèse underlines this word.

9. *LC* 189 in ibid., 1150.

had entrusted the helm of his spiritual life to her, and Thérèse had set him on a steady course, steering him to "enter into Love by means of confidence."[10] This way that she showed him has a name. This fortune that he inherited has a face. It was not an idea or a theory, but a Person—Jesus. He is the singular one whom Thérèse found all-sufficient—the pearl of great price for which she sold everything to gain all. Her conviction: "He who has Jesus has everything."[11] And Bellière gratefully acknowledges, "I found Him in you."[12]

By a most amazing conspiracy of grace, Maurice Bellière wrote for the last time to Thérèse on October 2, 1897. Unknown to him, Thérèse had already been called to the Lord on the evening of September 30. In his letter he celebrates the fact that he is now "a day-old missionary." On the previous day—the very date that would become Thérèse's feast in the Christian calendar, her "birthday" into glory—he had taken his missionary oath. In the moving lines of his letter he asks to whom this grace of his being a Christian evangelist, a herald of the Gospel, is really due. In the first place it is to Jesus. But after him there is no question as to whom Bellière feels he owes this remarkable grace:

> To my good little Sister of the Lisieux Carmel, Sister Thérèse of the Child Jesus.... I owe you this immense honor of being today the missionary of Jesus.[13]

For him and for many others after him, she unlocked "the way of simple and loving confidence"[14] as a sure path in following Jesus. Bold confidence is her charism—her abiding gift to the Church. Fearless trust is the essence of her spirit in which we desire to share—the *parrhesia* of which we all do well to seek a double por-

---

10. *LC* 191 in ibid., 1157.
11. The title of one of her poems: *Qui a Jésus a Tout, PN* 18 bis. in *OC,* 680.
12. *LC* 193 in *GC II,* 1171.
13. *LC* 201 in ibid., 1189–90.
14. *LT* 261 in ibid., 1165.

tion. Thérèse became for Bellière the principal protagonist of holy daring. This day-old missionary was in no doubt as to the exact nature of the precious inheritance he had received from the young woman of faith: "It is yourself."[15] Why should this legacy not be ours?

15. *LC* 201 in ibid., 1191.

BOOKS & MEDIA

The Daughters of St. Paul operate book and media centers at the following addresses. Visit, call or write the one nearest you today, or find us on the World Wide Web, www.pauline.org

CALIFORNIA

3908 Sepulveda Blvd, Culver City, CA 90230	310-397-8676
2640 Broadway Street, Redwood City, CA 94063	650-369-4230
5945 Balboa Avenue, San Diego, CA 92111	858-565-9181

FLORIDA

| 145 S.W. 107th Avenue, Miami, FL 33174 | 305-559-6715 |

HAWAII

| 1143 Bishop Street, Honolulu, HI 96813 | 808-521-2731 |
| Neighbor Islands call: | 866-521-2731 |

ILLINOIS

| 172 North Michigan Avenue, Chicago, IL 60601 | 312-346-4228 |

LOUISIANA

| 4403 Veterans Memorial Blvd, Metairie, LA 70006 | 504-887-7631 |

MASSACHUSETTS

| 885 Providence Hwy, Dedham, MA 02026 | 781-326-5385 |

MISSOURI

| 9804 Watson Road, St. Louis, MO 63126 | 314-965-3512 |

NEW JERSEY

| 561 U.S. Route 1, Wick Plaza, Edison, NJ 08817 | 732-572-1200 |

NEW YORK

| 150 East 52nd Street, New York, NY 10022 | 212-754-1110 |

PENNSYLVANIA

| 9171-A Roosevelt Blvd, Philadelphia, PA 19114 | 215-676-9494 |

SOUTH CAROLINA

| 243 King Street, Charleston, SC 29401 | 843-577-0175 |

TENNESSEE

| 4811 Poplar Avenue, Memphis, TN 38117 | 901-761-2987 |

TEXAS

| 114 Main Plaza, San Antonio, TX 78205 | 210-224-8101 |

VIRGINIA

| 1025 King Street, Alexandria, VA 22314 | 703-549-3806 |

CANADA

| 3022 Dufferin Street, Toronto, ON M6B 3T5 | 416-781-9131 |

¡También somos su fuente para libros,
videos y música en español!